YOUR KNOWLEDGE HAS VALUE

AF154440

- We will publish your bachelor's and master's thesis, essays and papers

- Your own eBook and book - sold worldwide in all relevant shops

- Earn money with each sale

Upload your text at www.GRIN.com and publish for free

Efficacy of Virtual Reality in Pain Management

Michael Fascia

Bibliographic information published by the German National Library:

The German National Library lists this publication in the National Bibliography; detailed bibliographic data are available on the Internet at http://dnb.dnb.de.

ISBN: 9783389044582
This book is also available as an ebook.

© GRIN Publishing GmbH
Trappentreustraße 1
80339 München

All rights reserved

Print and binding: Books on Demand GmbH, Norderstedt, Germany
Printed on acid-free paper from responsible sources.

The present work has been carefully prepared. Nevertheless, authors and publishers do not incur liability for the correctness of information, notes, links and advice as well as any printing errors.

GRIN web shop: https://www.grin.com/document/1488133

TECHNOLOGICAL EVOLUTION AND SOCIETAL SHIFTS

Dr Michael Fascia. Edinburgh Naoier University.

June 29, 2024

Contents

FOREWORD

The rapidly evolving technological landscape has had a profound impact on virtually every aspect of our lives, and education is no exception. In "Technological Evolution and Societal Shifts," Dr. Michael Fascia presents a comprehensive examination of how modern technology can transform educational systems, addressing both the potential benefits and the myriad challenges associated with integrating technology into learning environments. This work is particularly timely given the recent global shifts prompted by the COVID-19 pandemic. The sudden transition to remote learning has underscored the essential role of technology in education and highlighted the pressing need for educational systems to adapt to an increasingly digital world. The traditional model of education, with its standardized and often rigid approaches, is proving inadequate for preparing students for the complexities of the 21st century. Dr. Fascia's research provides a detailed exploration of how educational paradigms can evolve to better meet the needs of today's students through the thoughtful integration of technology.

Dr. Fascia emphasizes the importance of personalized learning environments made possible by advanced digital tools and adaptive software. These technologies enable educators to tailor learning experiences to individual student needs, thereby enhancing engagement and improving educational outcomes. The book explores various case studies, including Finland's innovative use of artificial intelligence in classrooms and Singapore's Smart Learning Spaces, to illustrate practical applications of technology that have led to significant improvements in student learning. However, the integration of technology in education is not without its challenges. Dr. Fascia addresses the critical issue of the digital divide, which exacerbates existing inequalities by limiting access to digital devices and reliable internet connectivity for underprivileged and rural communities. He advocates for policies that ensure equitable access to technology, comprehensive teacher training, and robust data privacy measures to protect student information. These measures are essential for creating an inclusive educational environment where all students can benefit from technological advancements. Moreover, this book provides a framework for integrating technology into education, emphasizing the need for a strategic and coordinated approach. This includes developing robust infrastructure, continuous professional development for educators, and policies that promote the integration of digital literacy into the curriculum. Dr. Fascia argues for the necessity of regular evaluations of technology integration efforts to assess their impact and identify areas for improvement.

In "Technological Evolution and Societal Shifts," Dr. Fascia not only explores the potential of technology to enhance learning but also delves into the broader implications for societal and economic systems. The ultimate vision presented is one of an education system that not only improves learning outcomes but also fosters critical thinking, creativity, and adaptability—skills indispensable for success in the global landscape of the 21st century. As we stand at the crossroads of educational reform and technological innovation, this work serves as a crucial guide for educators, policymakers, and stakeholders committed to harnessing the power of technology to create more effective, engaging, and equitable learning environments. Dr. Fascia's insights and recommendations provide a roadmap for transforming education to meet the challenges and opportunities of the future, ensuring that students are well-prepared to thrive in an interconnected and technologically advanced world.

Overview

In this work, we explore the transformative potential of technology in modern education systems, focusing on both the opportunities and challenges presented by rapid technological advancements. As education systems worldwide strive to adapt to dynamic global needs, technology offers tools that can significantly enhance the learning environment. The examination delves into the integration of technology in education, highlighting the creation of personalized learning environments through adaptive software and global connectivity, which facilitate cross-cultural exchanges and collaborative learning experiences among students on a global scale.

Comprehensive Analysis of the Digital Divide The book provides a comprehensive analysis of the digital divide, a significant barrier to equitable education. This divide, characterized by disparities in access to digital devices and reliable internet connectivity, exacerbates existing educational inequalities, particularly in underprivileged and rural areas. The analysis begins with a detailed exploration of the root causes of the digital divide, examining socioeconomic factors, geographic challenges, and infrastructural limitations that contribute to this disparity. The book discusses the multifaceted nature of the digital divide, noting how it not only affects students' ability to access educational resources but also impacts their overall academic performance and future opportunities. Examples of initiatives that address this gap include distributing laptops and tablets to students who cannot afford them, creating affordable or free internet access programs for low-income families, and deploying mobile education vans to remote communities. These mobile education vans are equipped with internet-enabled devices and educational resources, bringing digital learning tools directly to students who might otherwise be left behind. The discussion emphasizes the importance of ensuring that every student has the opportunity to benefit from technological advancements in education, regardless of their socioeconomic status or geographic location. We examine the role of public-private partnerships in addressing the digital divide. It highlights successful collaborations between governments, non-profit organizations, and technology companies that have resulted in increased access to digital tools and resources for students in underserved communities. By leveraging the strengths and resources of multiple stakeholders, these partnerships have created sustainable solutions to bridge the digital divide and promote digital equity. Another critical area explored is the necessity of comprehensive teacher training. The book advocates for professional development programs designed to equip teachers with both the technical proficiency to use educational technologies and the pedagogical strategies to integrate them into their teaching practices. These programs should cover a range of competencies, from basic digital literacy to advanced instructional technologies, and be flexible and accessible to accommodate the diverse needs of educators. The text underscores the importance of ongoing professional development to ensure that teachers are well-prepared to leverage technology to enhance student learning, and it highlights the role of supportive communities where teachers can share experiences and best practices.

We examine the specific components of effective teacher training programs, emphasizing the need for a holistic approach that combines theoretical knowledge with practical application. It discusses the importance of hands-on training sessions where teachers can experiment with new technologies in a controlled environment, receive feedback, and refine their skills. Additionally, the book highlights the value of mentorship and peer support networks, where experienced educators can provide guidance and share best practices with their colleagues. Furthermore, the book explores the impact of teacher training on student outcomes, presenting evidence from various studies that demonstrate the positive correlation between well-trained teachers and improved student performance. It discusses how teachers who are confident and proficient in using technology are better able to engage students, differentiate instruction, and create interactive and dynamic learning experiences.

Ensuring Data Privacy Ensuring data privacy is another critical component of successful technology integration. The increasing use of AI and other technologies in education involves the collection and analysis of vast amounts of personal data, raising significant concerns about data privacy. The book discusses the need for educational institutions to implement comprehensive data governance policies that prioritize the minimization of data collection, secure storage practices, and strict access controls. These policies should include clear guidelines on data usage and sharing, prohibiting the sale of student data to third parties and ensuring that any data sharing is done with explicit consent and for educational purposes only. The text highlights the importance of establishing robust data privacy measures to maintain trust and protect the rights of students. The book provides a detailed examination of the legal and ethical considerations surrounding data privacy in education. It explores existing regulations, such as the General Data Protection Regulation (GDPR) and the Family Educational Rights and Privacy Act (FERPA), and discusses how these laws apply to educational settings. The text also addresses the challenges of balancing data privacy with the need for data-driven decision-making in education, offering practical recommendations for achieving this balance. In addition to policy recommendations, we discusses the role of technology in enhancing data privacy. It explores the use of encryption, anonymization, and other technological solutions to protect student data and prevent unauthorized access. The text also emphasizes the importance of educating students, parents, and educators about data privacy and security, fostering a culture of awareness and vigilance.

Practical Applications of Technology in Education Various case studies from around the world illustrate practical applications of technology that have led to improved educational outcomes. Examples include Finland's use of artificial intelligence to personalize learning and Singapore's Smart Learning Spaces that leverage Internet of Things (IoT) technologies to create adaptable and responsive learning environments. These case studies demonstrate how diverse educational settings have successfully integrated technology to create more engaging, personalized, and effective learning experiences. The book provides an in-depth analysis of Finland's AI-driven education system, detailing how data analytics is used to tailor educational content to individual student needs. It discusses the algorithms and methodologies employed to analyze student performance data, identify learning gaps, and deliver customized instructional materials. The text also examines the impact of this personalized approach on student motivation, engagement, and academic achievement. In the case of Singapore's Smart Learning Spaces, the book explores how IoT technologies are used to create dynamic and interactive learning environments. It describes the various IoT devices and sensors deployed in classrooms to monitor student activity, assess learning conditions, and provide real-time feedback to teachers. The text highlights the benefits of this approach, including increased student engagement, improved classroom management, and enhanced learning outcomes. The text also presents additional case studies from countries such as the United States, Japan, and India, showcasing a wide range of technological innovations in education. These examples include the use of virtual reality for immersive learning experiences, blockchain for secure credentialing, and mobile apps for personalized learning pathways. Each case study is accompanied by an analysis of the implementation process, challenges encountered, and lessons learned.

Comprehensive Framework for Integrating Technology in Education The book outlines a comprehensive framework for integrating technology in education, advocating for a student-centered approach that employs technology to cater to individual learning styles and needs. The proposed framework emphasizes the development of robust infrastructure, pedagogical adaptation, and continuous professional development for educators. It suggests implementing adaptive learning technologies that use data to provide personalized learning experiences, helping to address the diverse needs of students and improve learning outcomes. The framework also includes strategies for monitoring, evaluation, and continuous improvement, with a robust system for tracking metrics such as standardized test scores, formative assessments, student engagement data, and feedback from both teachers and students. The book details the components of this framework, starting with infrastructure development. It discusses the importance of ensuring universal access to high-speed internet connectivity and providing adequate and up-to-date hardware and software solutions tailored to educational needs. The text explores various funding models and policy initiatives that can support infrastructure development, including government grants, public-private partnerships, and community-driven projects. Pedagogical adaptation is another key element of the framework and we discusses the need to rethink traditional teaching methods and incorporate digital literacy and critical thinking as core competencies. It presents various instructional strategies and models, such as blended learning, flipped classrooms, and project-based learning, that effectively integrate technology into the curriculum. The text also highlights the importance of fostering a culture of innovation and experimentation in schools, encouraging educators to explore new technologies and teaching approaches.

Strategies for Monitoring, Evaluation, and Continuous Improvement The framework also includes strategies for monitoring, evaluation, and continuous improvement. The book emphasizes the importance of establishing a robust system for tracking key metrics such as standardized test scores, formative assessments, student engagement data, and feedback from both teachers and students. It discusses the role of data analytics in identifying areas for improvement, refining instructional strategies, and making data-driven decisions regarding the selection and implementation of educational technologies. The text provides practical guidelines for setting up effective monitoring and evaluation systems, including the use of dashboards, reporting tools, and data visualization techniques. It also highlights the importance of creating feedback mechanisms that allow teachers and students to share their experiences and suggest improvements. By fostering a culture of continuous improvement, educational institutions can ensure that technology integration remains aligned with pedagogical goals and responds to the evolving needs of students. We further discuss various case studies of successful monitoring and evaluation practices, illustrating how different educational settings have effectively implemented these systems. It explores the challenges and best practices associated with data collection, analysis, and interpretation, providing valuable insights for educators and policymakers.

Policy Recommendations and Strategic Implementation Guidelines Conclusively, the book provides detailed policy recommendations and strategic implementation guidelines. It suggests that comprehensive planning, stakeholder engagement, and continuous evaluation are essential for realizing the full benefits of technology in education. The ultimate vision shared is an education system that utilizes technology not only to enhance learning outcomes but also to foster essential skills such as critical thinking, creativity, and adaptability, which are indispensable in the 21st-century global landscape. The book outlines a strategic roadmap for policymakers, detailing the steps needed to create an enabling environment for technology integration. It emphasizes the importance of stakeholder engagement, highlighting the roles of government agencies, educational institutions, technology providers, and the community in driving this transformation. The text also discusses the need for flexible and adaptive policy frameworks that can accommodate the rapid pace of technological change and address emerging challenges. By adopting a strategic approach to technology integration, educational institutions can create a learning environment that not only meets the current needs of students but also prepares them for the future. This includes fostering a culture of innovation and continuous learning, where technology is seen as a tool to enhance education rather than replace traditional teaching methods. The goal is to create an educational system that is flexible, inclusive, and capable of preparing students for the complexities of the modern world.

The book concludes with a call to action for educators, policymakers, and stakeholders to work collaboratively towards achieving this vision. It underscores the imperative of technological integration in education as a means to equip students for future challenges and opportunities, ensuring they are prepared to thrive in an interconnected and technologically advanced world.

Key Words. : Educational Technology, Personalized Learning, Adaptive Software, Digital Divide, Teacher Training, Global Connectivity, Technological Integration, Case Studies in Education

Introduction

As we navigate an era marked by rapid technological evolution and societal shifts, the role of education systems is increasingly under scrutiny. The onset of the COVID-19 pandemic has not only intensified existing challenges but also presented unique opportunities for reform. This work explores the intersection of technology and education, emphasizing the urgent need to prepare students for a future where both opportunities and uncertainties are magnified by technological advancements. The traditional model of education, largely unchanged for centuries, is proving inadequate in equipping students with the necessary skills and knowledge for the 21st century. The pandemic has highlighted the critical role of technology in education, propelling schools worldwide into remote learning scenarios almost overnight. This sudden shift has sparked a broader conversation about the potential of technology to transform educational paradigms. From personalized learning environments to global digital classrooms, technology offers unprecedented opportunities to tailor education to individual needs and global contexts. However, the integration of technology in education is not merely a logistical or pedagogical challenge; it is fundamentally a call to rethink the very purpose and methods of education. This work argues for a comprehensive reevaluation of educational systems, advocating for a transition from traditional, standardized approaches to more dynamic, student-centered learning frameworks that leverage technological tools to enhance learning outcomes and engagement. This transformative vision for education requires a departure from piecemeal reforms; instead, it demands a holistic reimagining of how education can harness the power of technology to foster not only academic skills but also critical thinking, creativity, and adaptability. Such a reformation is crucial not only for individual student success but also for societal progress in an increasingly complex global landscape. By examining the impact of technology on educational practices and the broader implications for societal and economic systems, this work sets the stage for a detailed exploration of how education can evolve to meet the demands of the future.

The following sections will consider specific technological advancements, their current and potential applications in education, and the policy and practical changes necessary to realize this vision

Technological Impact on Education

The integration of technology into education has significantly transformed learning environments, making them more adaptable and personalized. Recent advancements, accelerated by the necessity brought on by the COVID-19 pandemic, have highlighted the potential for technology to enhance educational delivery and outcomes. This section examines the critical roles of personalization and global connectivity facilitated by digital tools in reshaping education.

Personalization Through Technology

Personalized learning, facilitated by technological advancements, allows educational content, pacing, and learning strategies to be tailored to the individual needs of each student. Adaptive learning software, for instance, dynamically adjusts the difficulty of tasks based on a learner's performance, providing a custom-fit learning experience that can enhance student engagement and efficacy (Walker et al., 2020). Such technologies leverage data analytics to create a detailed understanding of a student's learning preferences, strengths, and areas for improvement, thereby fostering an environment where students can thrive at their own pace.

Examples and Applications:

- **Khan Academy and Coursera:** These platforms offer self-paced courses that students can navigate independently, with assessments that adapt based on the learner's performance. This method supports mastery learning and accommodates diverse learning styles and speeds, making education more inclusive and accessible (Smith et al., 2021).

- **Intelligent Tutoring Systems:** These systems use AI to provide immediate feedback and personalized instruction. For example, Carnegie Learning's MATHia adapts to each student's problem-solving approach, providing customized hints and problem sets.

- **Learning Management Systems (LMS):** Platforms like Moodle and Canvas allow educators to track student progress and adapt instructional materials to meet individual learning needs.

Impact on Student Engagement and Outcomes: Personalized learning enhances student motivation by aligning educational experiences with individual interests and needs. Research has shown that students engaged in personalized learning environments demonstrate higher levels of academic achievement and deeper understanding of the material (Pane et al., 2017).

Global Connectivity and Collaborative Learning

Technology also expands educational boundaries through global connectivity, enabling collaborative learning across different geographic locations. Online platforms facilitate interactions where students from various cultural backgrounds can engage in joint projects, share perspectives, and enhance their global awareness. Tools such as video conferencing software, online forums, and shared digital workspaces allow for real-time collaboration and communication, effectively creating a global classroom environment (Johnson & Adams Becker, 2017).

Examples and Applications:

- **Global Education Conference Network:** This initiative utilizes web-based technologies to bring together educators and students for collaborative learning activities that emphasize global citizenship (Global Education Conference, 2022).

- **ePals:** A platform that connects classrooms worldwide, allowing students to collaborate on projects, exchange cultural insights, and practice language skills.

- **Virtual Exchange Programs:** Programs like Soliya connect students from different countries to discuss global issues, promoting cross-cultural understanding and communication skills.

Impact on Educational Experience: Global connectivity fosters a more inclusive and culturally rich educational experience. It prepares students for an interconnected workforce by developing critical soft skills such as communication, collaboration, and cultural competence. Additionally, exposure to diverse perspectives enhances critical thinking and problem-solving abilities (Reimers et al., 2020).

Technological Implementation in Practice

Case Studies and Best Practices:

- **Finland's Education System:** Known for its innovative use of technology, Finland integrates AI and digital tools into the classroom to personalize learning and support student-centered teaching approaches.

- **Singapore's Smart Nation Initiative:** Singapore leverages technology to create Smart Learning Environments, incorporating digital tools and data analytics to enhance teaching and learning experiences.

Challenges and Considerations:

- **Digital Divide:** Ensuring equitable access to technology remains a significant challenge. Addressing infrastructure disparities and providing support for under-resourced schools are crucial steps.

- **Teacher Training:** Effective use of technology requires comprehensive professional development for educators to integrate digital tools into their teaching practices effectively.

- **Data Privacy and Security:** Implementing robust policies to protect student data and ensure secure use of educational technologies.

Future Directions in Educational Technology

Emerging Trends:

- **Artificial Intelligence and Machine Learning:** These technologies will continue to drive advancements in personalized learning, offering more sophisticated adaptive learning systems.

- **Augmented and Virtual Reality (AR/VR):** AR and VR are set to revolutionize experiential learning, providing immersive educational experiences that can enhance understanding and retention.

- **Blockchain for Education:** Blockchain technology holds potential for secure and transparent management of academic records, credentials, and assessments.

Policy Recommendations:

- **Investment in Infrastructure:** Governments and educational institutions should invest in reliable internet access and up-to-date hardware to support digital learning.

- **Professional Development:** Continuous training programs for teachers to keep abreast of technological advancements and integrate them effectively into the curriculum.

- **Inclusive Policies:** Developing policies that ensure all students, regardless of their background, have access to the benefits of educational technology.

Challenges and Opportunities in Technology-Driven Education

As educational systems increasingly adopt technological solutions, they encounter a complex array of challenges and opportunities. This section delves into the major hurdles that need to be addressed and the potential benefits that can be harnessed from a well-implemented technology-driven educational framework.

Addressing the Digital Divide

One of the most significant challenges in the widespread adoption of technology in education is the digital divide. This term refers to the gap between individuals who have easy access to the internet and computers and those who do not, which can exacerbate existing inequalities in education. According to a report by the United Nations Educational, Scientific and Cultural Organization (UNESCO), over 290 million students worldwide are impacted by this divide, hindering their ability to participate in digital learning environments (UNESCO, 2021). Efforts to bridge this divide must include not only the provision of hardware and internet access but also training for teachers and students to effectively use these technologies. Government and private sector partnerships are crucial in this endeavor, as they can facilitate the necessary investments in infrastructure and educational programs to ensure equitable access to technology. For instance, initiatives like India's mobile education vans have been pivotal in bringing internet-enabled devices and educational resources to remote and underserved communities. These vans not only provide the necessary hardware but also offer training sessions for teachers and students, ensuring they can effectively use these tools to enhance their learning experiences. Addressing the digital divide involves several critical components. First, providing physical resources such as computers, tablets, and reliable internet connections is essential. Many students in underserved areas lack access to these basic tools, which significantly hampers their ability to engage with digital learning materials. By equipping schools and community centers with the necessary technology, we can create more inclusive educational environments. Second, beyond mere access to hardware and the internet, there must be a focus on building digital literacy. This encompasses not only teaching students how to use technological tools but also integrating these tools into the curriculum in meaningful ways. Training programs for teachers are vital in this regard. Educators need to be adept at using technology to enhance learning, which includes understanding how to navigate educational software, implement digital assessments, and leverage online resources to support student learning. Ongoing professional development ensures that teachers remain up-to-date with the latest technological advancements and pedagogical strategies.

Furthermore, creating public-private partnerships can lead to sustainable models for providing continuous support and updates to technological infrastructure in schools. Companies in the tech industry can play a pivotal role by donating equipment, offering software solutions, and providing expertise in setting up robust digital learning environments. These collaborations can also extend to developing educational content and tools tailored to meet the specific needs of different student populations. Ensuring that rural and low-income areas receive adequate support is essential for minimizing the educational disparities that the digital divide can create. Government policies should prioritize funding for technology in these areas, ensuring that all students have the opportunity to benefit from digital learning. Programs like the U.S. Federal Communications Commission's (FCC) E-rate program, which provides discounts to help schools and libraries obtain affordable telecommunications and internet access, are examples of efforts to support connectivity in underserved regions. Additionally, community engagement plays a crucial role in addressing the digital divide. Local communities can support schools by providing spaces for digital learning labs, offering volunteer-led training sessions, and raising awareness about the importance of digital literacy. Community centers and libraries can serve as hubs for internet access and digital training, ensuring that students who may not have access to technology at home can still participate in digital learning. Efforts to bridge the digital divide must also consider the diverse needs of students. For instance, students with disabilities require adaptive technologies and accessible digital content to fully participate in online learning environments. Ensuring that educational technologies are designed with accessibility in mind is crucial for creating inclusive learning experiences. Finally, monitoring and evaluation are critical components of any initiative aimed at bridging the digital divide. Regular assessments of technology usage and effectiveness can help identify gaps and areas for improvement, ensuring that resources are used efficiently and equitably. Feedback from students, teachers, and parents can provide valuable insights into the challenges and successes of technology integration, guiding future efforts to enhance digital learning opportunities for all students. By addressing these various aspects of the digital divide, we can create a more equitable and effective educational landscape where all students have the opportunity to succeed in a technology-driven world.

Enhancing Teacher Training

The effectiveness of technology in education largely depends on the ability of educators to integrate new tools into their teaching practices. However, many teachers lack the necessary training to utilize these technologies effectively, which can limit the potential benefits of digital learning environments. Ongoing professional development and support systems are essential for educators to stay updated with the latest technological advancements and pedagogical strategies (Smith & Jones, 2020). Programs designed to enhance digital literacy among educators can lead to more innovative and effective teaching methodologies that fully exploit the capabilities of modern technology. For instance, teacher training initiatives that focus on integrating digital tools into the curriculum can foster more engaging and interactive classrooms. Training programs should be comprehensive, covering not only the use of specific software and hardware but also the pedagogical theories behind their use. Educators should learn how to design and implement technology-enhanced lesson plans that cater to various learning styles and needs. Institutions can adopt a blended learning approach to professional development, combining online courses with face-to-face workshops. This ensures that teachers have the flexibility to learn at their own pace while also benefiting from hands-on practice and peer collaboration. Additionally, creating a community of practice among educators can facilitate the sharing of best practices and continuous learning. Online forums and social media groups dedicated to educational technology can serve as platforms for teachers to exchange ideas, seek advice, and stay informed about the latest developments in the field.

Leveraging Technology for Inclusive Education

Technology has the potential to make education more inclusive by providing personalized learning experiences that cater to a wide range of learning needs and preferences. Tools such as speech-to-text software, reading assistants, and interactive learning modules can help address the diverse needs of students, including those with disabilities (Doe & Smith, 2019). For example, virtual reality (VR) can create immersive learning experiences for students with physical disabilities, allowing them to explore environments that would otherwise be inaccessible. Similarly, augmented reality (AR) can bring abstract concepts to life, providing visual and tactile learning aids that enhance understanding and retention for students with learning difficulties. Adaptive learning platforms can also play a crucial role in inclusive education by analyzing student data to tailor content delivery based on individual performance and learning preferences. This ensures that each student receives the appropriate level of challenge and support, maximizing their potential for success. In addition to technological tools, inclusive education also requires the development of policies and practices that support the diverse needs of students. This includes ensuring that digital content is accessible, with features such as subtitles for videos, alternative text for images, and customizable interfaces that allow students to adjust font sizes and color contrasts. Schools should also provide assistive technologies, such as screen readers and alternative input devices, to students who need them.

Expanding Learning Beyond Traditional Classrooms

The integration of technology in education opens up new possibilities for learning that transcend the limitations of traditional classroom settings. The advent of online platforms and e-learning tools has democratized access to education, allowing students to tap into a wealth of resources and opportunities regardless of their geographical location. This newfound flexibility not only supports lifelong learning but also fosters a more learner-centered approach, enabling students to pursue their interests and career goals at their own pace and according to their individual needs (Global Learning Council, 2021). E-learning platforms such as Coursera, edX, and Khan Academy have revolutionized the educational landscape by offering courses on a vast array of subjects. These platforms bridge gaps in traditional education by providing content that may not be covered in standard school curricula. They offer video lectures from top-tier educators, interactive quizzes to reinforce learning, and peer discussion forums that facilitate collaborative learning and critical thinking. These platforms operate on a model of accessibility and inclusivity. Coursera and edX, for instance, partner with leading universities and institutions to offer Massive Open Online Courses (MOOCs). MOOCs democratize education by making high-quality, university-level courses available to anyone with an internet connection, often at no cost. This model is particularly beneficial for learners in remote or underserved areas who may not have access to advanced educational opportunities otherwise. The flexibility provided by e-learning platforms supports a more personalized learning experience. Students can engage with course materials at their own pace, revisiting complex topics as needed and accelerating through areas where they are already proficient. This approach not only enhances understanding but also reduces the pressure and anxiety often associated with traditional classroom environments. Personalization extends beyond pacing. Adaptive learning technologies, which many e-learning platforms incorporate, tailor the learning experience to individual student needs. These technologies use algorithms to analyze a learner's performance and adapt content accordingly, ensuring that each student receives the right level of challenge and support. This method enhances engagement and effectiveness, as learners are neither bored by material that is too easy nor overwhelmed by content that is too difficult. Blended learning models, which combine online and face-to-face instruction, represent a significant innovation in educational delivery. These models harness the best of both worlds, offering the flexibility of online learning with the interactive benefits of traditional classroom experiences. Students can complete theoretical components of a course online, allowing them to absorb and reflect on content at their own pace. Subsequently, they participate in hands-on labs or discussions in the classroom, where they can apply their knowledge and engage in deeper, more interactive learning experiences. For instance, in a science course, students might watch video lectures and complete online simulations at home, then come to class prepared to engage in lab experiments or group discussions. This approach not only maximizes instructional time but also encourages active learning and critical thinking. Moreover, blended learning accommodates diverse learning styles and needs, making education more inclusive. The flexibility and accessibility of e-learning platforms support lifelong learning and continuous professional development. As the job market evolves, individuals can leverage these platforms to acquire new skills, stay current with industry trends, and advance their careers. This is particularly important in fast-paced fields such as technology and healthcare, where ongoing education is essential. For example, professionals can enroll in online courses to earn certifications in new technologies or methodologies relevant to their fields. Employers can also use these platforms to provide employee training and development programs, ensuring their workforce remains competitive and well-equipped to handle emerging challenges. Despite the numerous benefits, the integration of technology in education must address certain barriers to ensure equitable access. The digital divide remains a significant challenge, as not all students have reliable access to the internet or digital devices. Efforts to bridge this divide are essential for ensuring that all students can benefit from the opportunities provided by online and blended learning models. Governments and educational institutions can collaborate with private sector partners to invest in infrastructure and provide necessary resources to underserved communities. Initiatives like mobile learning labs and community internet access points can help reach students in remote areas, ensuring they have the tools and connectivity needed to participate in digital learning environments.

Case Studies of Successful Technological Integration in Education

To illustrate the practical application and benefits of technology in education, this section examines several case studies from around the world. These examples highlight how diverse educational settings have successfully implemented technology to enhance learning experiences and outcomes. The practical application and benefits of educational technology can be observed through a multitude of case studies from diverse global settings. These examples illustrate how various educational systems have successfully leveraged technology to create more engaging, personalized, and effective learning experiences.

Finland's Digital Education Revolution

Finland, renowned for its high-performing educational system, has embraced a comprehensive approach to technology integration. A pilot project in Helsinki schools introduced artificial intelligence (AI) to personalize learning and boost student engagement (Nordic Innovation, 2022). The AI system analyzes individual student learning patterns, providing tailored recommendations for both students and teachers. This data-driven approach allows teachers to identify students who may need additional support and adjust their pedagogical strategies accordingly, ultimately improving student performance and engagement (Kahoot!, 2019). The Finnish model serves as a compelling example of how AI can transform education by facilitating personalized learning paths and offering actionable insights to educators.

Singapore's Smart Learning Spaces

Singapore's innovative "Smart Learning Spaces" leverage Internet of Things (IoT) technologies to create adaptable and responsive learning environments (Ministry of Education, Singapore, 2021). These classrooms are equipped with sensors and smart devices that adjust lighting, temperature, and even rearrange physical layouts to optimize learning for different activities and teaching styles. The technology also incorporates real-time feedback systems, enabling students to interact with educational content dynamically and allowing teachers to monitor engagement and comprehension continuously. This initiative has fostered a more conducive and personalized learning environment, enhancing the overall educational experience and demonstrating the potential of IoT to revolutionize classroom design and instruction.

Rural India's Mobile Education Vans

In rural India, where access to quality education and technological infrastructure can be limited, mobile education vans have emerged as a transformative solution. These vans, equipped with computers, internet access, and educational technology tools, travel to remote areas to provide children with access to digital learning resources and online courses (Digital India, 2022). This initiative has significantly expanded educational outreach, enabling children in underserved areas to access the same educational opportunities as their urban counterparts. By overcoming geographical and socio-economic barriers, mobile education vans have demonstrated the potential of mobile technology to democratize education and bridge the digital divide.

The United States' Blended Learning Programs

The United States has seen a growing adoption of blended learning programs that combine online digital media with traditional classroom methods. The Rocketship Public Schools network is a prime example, employing a rotational model where students alternate between engaging with digital content and receiving in-person instruction from teachers (Rocketship, 2021). This approach enables personalized instruction, allowing teachers to focus on small group interactions and tailor their teaching to individual student needs. Research has shown that blended learning models, like the one implemented by Rocketship, can lead to significant improvements in test scores and student comprehension, particularly in math and reading skills (Means et al., 2010).

These case studies collectively illustrate the diverse ways in which educational technology can be harnessed to enhance learning experiences and outcomes. From personalized learning powered by AI to adaptive learning environments and mobile solutions for underserved communities, these examples showcase the transformative potential of technology in education when implemented thoughtfully and strategically.

Framework for Integrating Technology in Education

Section 5 of the framework for integrating technology in education provides a comprehensive approach that incorporates modal logic and Bayesian probability to enhance the decision-making process across key areas: infrastructure, teacher training, curriculum adaptation, student-centric strategies, monitoring, evaluation, and inclusivity. By employing necessity and possibility operators alongside Bayesian updates, we quantitatively analyze and improve the reliability of infrastructure, the effectiveness of teacher training, the integration of technology into pedagogy, and the robustness of monitoring systems. These probabilistic methods yield a deeper understanding of the conditions necessary for successful technology integration and highlight potential areas for improvement. Enhanced analytical precision further ensures that educational practices not only meet current needs but are also adaptable to future challenges, thus fostering a culture of continuous improvement and equity in education. This structured, data-driven approach significantly strengthens the framework's capacity to support effective and inclusive educational environments. To fully harness the transformative potential of technology in education, a robust and adaptable framework is essential. This framework should encompass three interconnected pillars: infrastructure and accessibility, teacher training and professional development, and curriculum integration and pedagogical adaptation.

Establishing Infrastructure and Accessibility

The foundation of any successful technology integration initiative lies in establishing a robust and reliable infrastructure. This entails ensuring universal access to high-speed internet connectivity, providing adequate and up-to-date hardware such as laptops, tablets, and interactive whiteboards, and procuring software solutions specifically tailored to educational needs. Governments and educational institutions must prioritize substantial investments in building and maintaining this technological backbone, as it is a prerequisite for effective digital learning environments. For instance, research indicates that a lack of reliable internet access significantly hinders the implementation of online learning platforms and digital resources, particularly in rural and underserved areas (Warschauer, 2016). Initiatives like India's mobile education vans, which bring internet-enabled devices and educational resources to remote communities, offer a promising model for bridging the digital divide and ensuring equitable access to technology (Digital India, 2022).

Beyond mere access, the infrastructure must also be designed for scalability and adaptability to accommodate future technological advancements. This may involve cloud-based solutions, modular hardware upgrades, and software platforms that can be easily customized and updated. A scalable infrastructure not only ensures that technology can be expanded to reach a wider audience but also allows for seamless integration of new tools and resources as they emerge.

Modal Logic Application:

- **Necessity (A):** Reliable high-speed internet is a necessary condition (A) for the effectiveness of online learning platforms.

- **Possibility ():** There is a possibility (b) that integrating satellite internet technology could enhance connectivity in geographically challenging areas.

Bayesian Probability Analysis:

- **Prior Probability (P):** Suppose the initial belief in the adequacy of current infrastructure is 70% (0.70).

- **Likelihood (L):** The likelihood that we observe successful integration given the current infrastructure state is 80% (0.80).

- **Posterior Probability (P'):** Using Bayesian update to reassess the belief in infrastructure adequacy after observing integration success.

Bayesian Update Formula:

-
$$P(\text{adequate} \mid \text{success}) = \frac{P(\text{success} \mid \text{adequate}) \cdot P(\text{adequate})}{P(\text{success})}$$

- Calculating the denominator via the Total Probability Theorem:

$$P(\text{success}) = P(\text{success} \mid \text{adequate}) \cdot P(\text{adequate}) + P(\text{success} \mid \text{inadequate}) \cdot P(\text{inadequate})$$

- Assuming $P(\text{success} \mid \text{inadequate}) = 30\%$ (0.30), and $P(\text{inadequate}) = 1 - P(\text{adequate}) = 30\%$ (0.30),

-
$$P(\text{success}) = (0.80 \cdot 0.70) + (0.30 \cdot 0.30) = 0.56 + 0.09 = 0.65$$

-
$$P(\text{adequate} \mid \text{success}) = \frac{0.80 \cdot 0.70}{0.65} \approx 0.86 \ (86\%)$$

$P(\text{a}) = 0.70$ Adequate   Success

$P(\text{inadequate}) = 0.30$ Inadequate

This updated probability (86%) reflects an increased confidence in the infrastructure's adequacy following the observed success, underscoring the importance of continuous data-driven adjustments in our approach to technology integration in education.

Teacher Training and Professional Development

Equipping educators with the necessary skills and knowledge to effectively leverage technology in their teaching practices is paramount. Continuous professional development programs should be a cornerstone of any technology integration initiative. These programs should provide teachers with comprehensive training in the latest educational technologies, pedagogical strategies tailored for digital and blended learning environments, and data literacy skills to interpret and utilize student performance data. Research suggests that teacher training significantly impacts the successful integration of technology in the classroom, influencing teachers' attitudes, confidence, and ability to effectively use technology to enhance student learning (Lawless & Pellegrino, 2007).

Finland's approach to utilizing AI for personalized learning provides an inspiring example of effective teacher training (Nordic Innovation, 2022). The program focuses on equipping teachers with the skills to interpret and act on data-driven insights, enabling them to tailor instruction to individual student needs and maximize learning outcomes. By investing in teacher training, educational institutions can empower educators to become facilitators of technology-enhanced learning, fostering a culture of innovation and continuous improvement.

Curriculum Integration and Pedagogical Adaptation

To fully realize the potential of educational technology, it must be seamlessly integrated into the curriculum and pedagogical practices. This involves a fundamental shift in how we think about teaching and learning, moving away from traditional lecture-based models towards more student-centered, active learning approaches. The curriculum should be redesigned to incorporate digital literacy as a core competency, equipping students with the skills to critically evaluate information, collaborate effectively online, and create digital content. Technological tools should not be viewed as mere supplements to traditional instruction but as integral components of the learning process. Interactive simulations, virtual field trips, online collaboration platforms, and adaptive learning software can all be leveraged to create engaging and personalized learning experiences. Singapore's Smart Learning Spaces offer a glimpse into the future of education, where technology is seamlessly integrated into the physical learning environment, fostering collaboration, creativity, and critical thinking (Ministry of Education, Singapore, 2021).

Modal Logic Application:

- **Necessity (A)**: Integrating critical thinking and digital literacy into the curriculum is necessary (A) for preparing students to navigate the digital world effectively.

- **Possibility (b)**: There is a possibility (b) that augmented reality tools could revolutionize the teaching of complex scientific and historical concepts.

Bayesian Probability Analysis:

- **Prior Probability (P):** Initial belief about the effectiveness of traditional pedagogical methods, say 0.60.
- **Likelihood (L):** Given the integration of digital tools, the probability of observing enhanced student engagement and learning outcomes, say 0.90.
- **Posterior Probability (P'):** Reassessing the effectiveness of pedagogical strategies post-integration.

Bayesian Update Formula:

-

$$P(\text{effective pedagogy} \mid \text{observed engagement}) = \frac{P(\text{oe} \mid \text{ep}) \cdot P(\text{effective pedagogy})}{P(\text{observed engagement})}$$

- Assuming

$$P(\text{observed engagement} \mid \text{ineffective pedagogy}) = 0.40,$$

- Calculating the denominator via the Total Probability Theorem:

$$P(\text{observed engagement}) = P(\text{oe} \mid \text{ep}) \cdot P(\text{effective pedagogy}) + P(\text{oe} \mid \text{ip}) \cdot P(\text{ineffective pedagogy})$$

- Given

$$P(\text{effective pedagogy}) = 0.60 \quad \text{and} \quad P(\text{ineffective pedagogy}) = 1 - P(\text{effective pedagogy}) = 0.40,$$

- We have

$$P(\text{observed engagement}) = (0.90 \cdot 0.60) + (0.40 \cdot 0.40) = 0.54 + 0.16 = 0.70,$$

- Therefore,

$$P(\text{effective pedagogy} \mid \text{observed engagement}) = \frac{0.90 \cdot 0.60}{0.70} \approx 0.77 \ (77\%)$$

This updated probability (77) indicates a higher confidence in the effectiveness of integrated pedagogical methods, underscoring the impact of technology on learning outcomes.

Student-Centric Approaches

The framework should prioritize student-centric approaches that cater to diverse learning styles and needs, recognizing that learners have unique preferences, strengths, and weaknesses. Adaptive learning technologies, which leverage artificial intelligence and machine learning algorithms to personalize instruction based on individual student performance and preferences, have emerged as a promising tool in this regard. These technologies can dynamically adjust the content, pacing, and difficulty of learning materials to match each student's abilities and interests. Moreover, tools that provide immediate feedback and allow for self-paced learning empower students to take ownership of their educational journeys, fostering self-regulation and metacognition (Hattie & Timperley, 2007). This personalized approach not only enhances student engagement and motivation but also promotes deeper understanding and improved academic outcomes.

Modal Logic and Bayesian Analysis for Remaining Sections: Sections 5.5 (Monitoring, Evaluation, and Continuous Improvement) and 5.6 (Inclusion and Equity) will similarly incorporate modal logic to delineate necessary and possible improvements, and use Bayesian probability to provide a granular, data-driven analysis of the effectiveness of monitoring strategies and the inclusive nature of educational technology. Each section will feature calculations that align with the initial beliefs, observed data, and resultant updates to those beliefs, ensuring a comprehensive understanding of the impact and areas for future enhancement.

Monitoring, Evaluation, and Continuous Improvement

To ensure the effectiveness and sustainability of technology integration efforts, a robust monitoring and evaluation system is essential. This system should track a range of metrics, including standardized test scores, formative assessments, student engagement data, and feedback from both teachers and students. By collecting and analyzing data on how students interact with technology and how it impacts their learning, educators can gain valuable insights into the strengths and weaknesses of their approaches. Regular assessments of these metrics enable institutions to identify areas for improvement, refine instructional strategies, and make data-driven decisions regarding the selection and implementation of educational technologies. Additionally, feedback mechanisms that allow teachers and students to share their experiences and suggest improvements foster a culture of continuous improvement and ensure that technology remains aligned with pedagogical goals.

Modal Logic Application:

- **Necessity (A)**: Regular data collection and analysis are necessary (A) for the continuous improvement of educational practices.
- **Possibility (b)**: There is a possibility (b) that implementing advanced analytics tools could significantly enhance the precision of performance assessments.

Bayesian Probability Analysis:

- **Prior Probability (P)**: Initial belief in the adequacy of existing evaluation methods, say 0.50.
- **Likelihood (L)**: Given new analytics tools, the probability of accurately measuring educational outcomes increases to 0.95.

- **Posterior Probability (P')**: Updated belief in the effectiveness of evaluation methods after implementing advanced tools.

Bayesian Update Formula:

- P'(effective evaluation | new tools) = [P(new tools | effective evaluation) * P(effective evaluation)] / P(new tools)
- Assuming P(new tools | ineffective evaluation) = 0.30,
- P(new tools) = (0.95 * 0.50) + (0.30 * 0.50) = 0.475 + 0.15 = 0.625
- P'(effective evaluation | new tools) = (0.95 * 0.50) / 0.625 -= 0.76 (76%)

This updated probability demonstrates an increased confidence in the evaluation methods, suggesting that new analytical tools have a substantial impact on the precision of assessments.

Inclusion and Equity

Ensuring that all students, regardless of their socioeconomic background, have equitable access to technology-enhanced education is a critical ethical imperative. This involves not only providing hardware and software but also addressing issues related to digital literacy, language barriers, and cultural relevance. Initiatives like the International Society for Technology in Education's (ISTE) Standards for Students emphasize the importance of equity and cultural responsiveness in technology integration. Provisions for students with disabilities, such as assistive technologies and accessible learning materials, are also essential to create an inclusive digital learning environment. To achieve this, collaboration among stakeholders across all levels of education is essential. Policymakers, school administrators, teachers, community leaders, and technology providers must work together to create policies, allocate resources, and develop programs that promote equitable access to technology and support for all learners.

Modal Logic Application:

- **Necessity (A)**: Equitable access to technology is a necessary condition (A) for achieving fairness in education.
- **Possibility (b)**: There is a possibility (b) that new funding models and community partnerships could effectively address disparities in technology access.

Bayesian Probability Analysis:

- **Prior Probability (P)**: Initial belief in the current level of equity in technology access, say 0.55.
- **Likelihood (L)**: With new initiatives and partnerships, the probability of achieving true equity increases to 0.85.

- **Posterior Probability (P′)**: Updated belief in the level of equity after implementing new strategies.

Bayesian Update Formula:

- P′(equity achieved | new initiatives) = [P(new initiatives | equity achieved) * P(equity achieved)] / P(new initiatives)
- Assuming P(new initiatives | not achieved) = 0.40,
- P(new initiatives) = (0.85 * 0.55) + (0.40 * 0.45) = 0.4675 + 0.18 = 0.6475
- P′(equity achieved | new initiatives) = (0.85 * 0.55) / 0.6475 -= 0.73 (73%)

This analysis shows that implementing targeted initiatives significantly improves the probability of achieving equitable access, supporting the need for ongoing, data-informed efforts to enhance inclusion in educational technology.

Implementation Strategies and Policy Recommendations

Implementing a technology-driven educational framework requires comprehensive strategies that align with policy recommendations to ensure sustainable and effective integration. This section outlines key strategies and policy measures that educational systems can adopt to facilitate the successful implementation of technology in education.

The successful integration of technology in education hinges on comprehensive strategies that align with well-defined policy recommendations, ensuring a sustainable and effective transformation of the learning landscape. These strategies must address a multifaceted array of challenges, encompassing infrastructure, pedagogy, professional development, equity, and long-term sustainability.

Strategic Planning and Stakeholder Engagement

Effective implementation of educational technology requires a collaborative and strategic approach, involving all stakeholders in the planning process. This group includes government bodies, educational institutions, technology providers, teachers, students, and parents. By integrating diverse perspectives and expertise, the solutions implemented can be precisely tailored to meet the specific needs and constraints of each educational system. For instance, Finland's integration of AI in classrooms involved extensive consultations with educators to ensure alignment with pedagogical goals and maximize the effectiveness of the technology (Nordic Innovation, 2022). The involvement of students and parents is crucial as their feedback on user preferences and accessibility issues can significantly enhance the adoption and utility of technological tools.

Detailed Analysis and Application of Bayesian Probability:

Objective Setting and Stakeholder Analysis: Strategic planning begins with defining clear, actionable objectives that are aligned with the broader educational goals. It is essential to identify all stakeholders and understand their influence and interest in the project, ranging from direct influencers like teachers and IT staff to indirect influencers like parents and students.

Resource Allocation and Risk Management: Resource allocation covers budgeting, scheduling, and human resources, ensuring that funding is available and timelines are suitable for training and implementation without disrupting academic activities. Risk management involves identifying potential risks—technical, financial, or user adoption-related—and developing strategies to mitigate these risks.

Performance Metrics and Continuous Evaluation: Performance metrics are established to monitor technology usage, engagement rates, and educational outcomes. These metrics provide a basis for continuous evaluation, allowing for adjustments in strategy based on observed results.

To support strategic decisions in educational technology implementation, we update our beliefs about the success of the integration based on new evidence of stakeholder satisfaction:

Prior Probability (P): Let's start with an initial belief about the success rate of technology integration. Assume $P(\text{Success}) = 0.70$ (70%).

Likelihood (L): Suppose the probability of observing current stakeholder satisfaction given successful technology integration is high, set at $P(\text{Satisfaction} \mid \text{Success}) = 0.90$ (90%).

Calculate P(Satisfaction):

- This is the total probability of observing satisfaction from all possible success states.
- Assume the probability of observing satisfaction when the integration is not successful is $P(\text{Satisfaction} \mid \text{Not Success}) = 0.30$ (30%).
- Compute the total probability of satisfaction:
  - $P(\text{Satisfaction}) = (P(\text{Satisfaction} \mid \text{Success}) * P(\text{Success})) + (P(\text{Satisfaction} \mid \text{Not Success}) * P(\text{Not Success}))$
  - $P(\text{Satisfaction}) = (0.90 * 0.70) + (0.30 * 0.30) = 0.63 + 0.09 = 0.72$

Posterior Probability (P'):

- Update the belief in success after observing satisfaction using the Bayesian update formula:
  - $P'(\text{Success} \mid \text{Satisfaction}) = (P(\text{Satisfaction} \mid \text{Success}) * P(\text{Success})) / P(\text{Satisfaction})$
  - $P'(\text{Success} \mid \text{Satisfaction}) = (0.90 * 0.70) / 0.72 -= 0.875$

- This result, P'(Success | Satisfaction) -= 0.875 or 87.5%, represents the updated belief in the success of the technology integration following the positive stakeholder feedback. This higher confidence level suggests that the integration is likely succeeding as stakeholders are satisfied, thereby justifying further investment and continuation along the current strategic path.

Policy Development and Funding

Governments play a pivotal role in fostering technology integration through the development of clear and comprehensive policies. These policies should encompass guidelines for data privacy, robust funding models, and strategic infrastructure development initiatives. Additionally, policies must explicitly address equity issues to prevent the exacerbation of the digital divide. Substantial and sustained investments are required to build and maintain the digital infrastructure necessary for modern learning environments, as demonstrated by Singapore's Smart Learning Spaces initiative, which has successfully integrated technology across the nation's schools through substantial government funding (Ministry of Education, Singapore, 2021).

Detailed Discussion and Probabilistic Analysis:

Policy Framework Development: Developing a policy framework involves drafting, reviewing, and enforcing guidelines that govern the use of technology in educational settings. This includes data privacy laws to protect student information, regulations on technology procurement, and standards for online content.

Funding Strategies: Funding is critical to support the widespread adoption and sustained use of educational technology. Strategies include direct government funding, grants, public-private partnerships, and incentives for schools that successfully implement technology programs. These financial strategies ensure that resources are allocated efficiently and equitably to support educational technology initiatives.

Equity Considerations: Policies must ensure that all students have equal access to technology-enhanced learning. This involves providing resources to underserved communities and adapting technologies to meet diverse needs, including those of students with disabilities.

Probabilistic Calculation for Funding Adequacy:

To assess the adequacy of funding and the likelihood of meeting the policy goals, we can use a simple probabilistic model:

Prior Probability (P): Let's assume the initial belief in the adequacy of funding based on current budget allocations is P(Adequate Funding) = 0.60 (60%).

Likelihood (L): Suppose new funding measures are introduced, and we estimate the probability of observing policy success given adequate funding is P(Success | Adequate Funding) = 0.80 (80%).

Total Probability of Success (P(Success)):

- Assume the probability of policy success when funding is not adequate is lower, P(Success | Not Adequate Funding) = 0.40 (40%).
- Compute the total probability of policy success:
  - P(Success) = (P(Success | Adequate Funding) * P(Adequate Funding)) + (P(Success | Not Adequate Funding) * (1 - P(Adequate Funding)))
  - P(Success) = (0.80 * 0.60) + (0.40 * 0.40) = 0.48 + 0.16 = 0.64

Posterior Probability (P'):

- Update the belief in the adequacy of funding after observing policy success:
  - P'(Adequate Funding | Success) = (P(Success | Adequate Funding) * P(Adequate Funding)) / P(Success)
  - P'(Adequate Funding | Success) = (0.80 * 0.60) / 0.64 -= 0.75
- This result, P'(Adequate Funding | Success) -= 0.75 or 75%, represents the updated belief in the adequacy of funding given the observed success of the policies. This improved confidence level suggests that the new funding strategies are likely effective, supporting the continuation and possibly an expansion of these initiatives.

This method provides a quantifiable means to evaluate the effectiveness of funding models in achieving educational technology policy goals, enabling data-driven adjustments to ensure all initiatives are supported adequately and equitably.

Professional Development and Support Systems

Effective utilization of educational technology hinges on educators' capacity to integrate new tools and methodologies into their teaching practices. Ongoing professional development programs are essential to equip teachers with the necessary skills and knowledge to navigate the ever-evolving digital landscape. These programs should not only focus on technical proficiency but also on pedagogical strategies for leveraging technology to enhance student learning outcomes. Robust support systems, including dedicated technical support staff and instructional designers, are vital to assist teachers in troubleshooting technical issues and creating engaging digital content.

Detailed Analysis and Complex Probabilistic Calculations Using Sets:

Development of Professional Development Programs: Professional development programs should be comprehensive, covering a range of competencies from basic digital literacy to advanced instructional technologies. These programs ensure that all teachers, regardless of their initial skill levels, can effectively implement technology in their classrooms.

Support System Structure: Support systems must include both reactive support (help desks, technical troubleshooting) and proactive support (workshops, online resources, and community practice groups). These elements form a network of resources that teachers can rely on to continuously improve their technological and pedagogical skills.

Complex Probabilistic Calculations Using Sets: To evaluate the effectiveness of professional development programs, we consider the set of all teachers T and define subsets based on their engagement with professional development and subsequent performance improvements.

Sets Defined:

- Let A be the set of teachers who participate in professional development.
- Let B be the set of teachers who demonstrate significant improvements in integrating technology into their teaching.

Probabilities Defined:

- $P(A)$: Probability that a randomly selected teacher has participated in professional development.
- $P(B)$: Probability that a randomly selected teacher has improved in technology integration.
- $P(B \mid A)$: Probability that a teacher improves given that they have participated in professional development.

Calculate P(B) Using Total Probability Theorem:

- Assume $P(B \mid A) = 0.85$ and $P(B \mid A^c) = 0.30$, where A^c is the complement of set A, representing teachers who did not participate.
- $P(A) = 0.75$ (75% of teachers participate in professional development).
- **Total Probability Calculation:**
  - $P(B) = P(B \mid A) * P(A) + P(B \mid A^c) * P(A^c)$
  - $P(B) = 0.85 * 0.75 + 0.30 * 0.25 = 0.6375 + 0.075 = 0.7125$

Bayesian Update for P(A | B) (Posterior Probability):

- Update the probability that a teacher who has improved is one who participated in professional development.
- $P(A \mid B) = (P(B \mid A) * P(A)) / P(B)$
- $P(A \mid B) = (0.85 * 0.75) / 0.7125 -= 0.893$

This calculation indicates that approximately 89.3% of teachers who show significant improvements are those who participated in professional development. This strong correlation underscores the effectiveness of these programs and justifies further investments and enhancements in professional development and support systems.

Curriculum and Assessment Redesign

To fully harness the potential of educational technology, a comprehensive redesign of curricula and assessment methods is imperative. Curricula should be updated to incorporate digital literacy skills, critical thinking, and problem-solving as core competencies, reflecting the demands of the 21st-century workforce. Assessment methods should evolve to measure not only content knowledge but also the digital skills and competencies students develop through technology-enhanced learning. The Rocketship Public Schools network's successful implementation of blended learning models demonstrates how curricula and assessments can be adapted to leverage technology effectively, resulting in improved student engagement and achievement (Rocketship, 2021).

Detailed Analysis and Probabilistic Evaluation:

- **Curriculum Integration:** Incorporate digital tools that facilitate interactive learning environments, such as simulations and collaborative platforms.

- **Assessment Innovation:** Transition to digital assessments that can dynamically adapt to the student's ability level in real-time, providing more accurate and timely evaluations.

Probabilistic Analysis of Implementation Success:

- **Prior Probability (P):** Assume the initial belief in the successful adaptation of curricula is P(Successful Adaptation) = 0.65 (65%).

- **Likelihood (L):** Given new training and resources, the probability of observing successful adaptation is P(Adaptation Success | New Resources) = 0.80 (80%).

Calculate the total probability of adaptation success:

- **P(Success):** Assume the probability of success without new resources is P(Adaptation Success | No New Resources) = 0.30 (30%).

- **Total Probability Calculation:**
  - P(Success) = (P(Adaptation Success | New Resources) * P(Successful Adaptation)) + (P(Adaptation Success | No New Resources) * (1 - P(Successful Adaptation)))
  - P(Success) = (0.80 * 0.65) + (0.30 * 0.35) = 0.52 + 0.105 = 0.625

Update the belief in successful adaptation after observing positive outcomes:

- **Posterior Probability (P'):**

  - P'(Successful Adaptation | Success) = (P(Adaptation Success | New Resources) * P(Successful Adaptation)) / P(Success)

  - P'(Successful Adaptation | Success) = (0.80 * 0.65) / 0.625 -= 0.832

This updated belief of approximately 83.2% suggests a higher confidence in the successful adaptation of curricula following the introduction of new resources and training.

Monitoring, Evaluation, and Feedback Loops

A robust monitoring and evaluation framework is crucial to assess the impact of technology integration on educational outcomes and inform ongoing improvement efforts. This framework should include mechanisms for collecting feedback from all stakeholders, including students, teachers, administrators, parents, and community members. This feedback loop can identify areas for improvement and guide adjustments to technology infrastructure and educational programs, ensuring their continued relevance and effectiveness (Global Learning Council, 2021).

Detailed Monitoring Framework and Probabilistic Updates:

- **Data Collection Points:** Establish specific metrics for engagement, learning outcomes, and system usability.

- **Stakeholder Feedback:** Regularly collect and analyze feedback from all stakeholders to identify strengths and areas for improvement.

- **Adaptive Learning Technologies:** Use data from learning management systems to adjust educational content and teaching methods in real-time, catering to the evolving needs of students.

Probabilistic Analysis of Feedback Integration:

- **Prior Probability (P):** Assume the initial belief in the effectiveness of feedback mechanisms is P(Effective Feedback) = 0.70 (70%).

- **Likelihood (L):** Given the implementation of comprehensive data collection, the probability of effective feedback is P(Effective Feedback | Comprehensive Data Collection) = 0.85 (85%).

Calculate the total probability of effective feedback:

- **P(Effective Feedback):** Assume the probability of effectiveness without comprehensive data collection is P(Effective Feedback | No Data Collection) = 0.40 (40%).

- **Total Probability Calculation:**

- P(Feedback) = (P(Effective Feedback | Comprehensive Data Collection) * P(Effective Feedback)) + (P(Effective Feedback | No Data Collection) * (1 - P(Effective Feedback)))

- P(Feedback) = (0.85 * 0.70) + (0.40 * 0.30) = 0.595 + 0.12 = 0.715

Update the belief in the effectiveness of feedback mechanisms after observing successful integration:

- **Posterior Probability (P'):**

  - P'(Effective Feedback | Feedback) = (P(Effective Feedback | Comprehensive Data Collection) * P(Effective Feedback)) / P(Feedback)

  - P'(Effective Feedback | Feedback) = (0.85 * 0.70) / 0.715 -= 0.832

This result, approximately 83.2%, indicates a high level of confidence in the effectiveness of feedback mechanisms when comprehensive data collection is implemented.

Ensuring Accessibility and Inclusion

The promise of educational technology can only be fully realized when it is accessible to all learners, regardless of their socioeconomic background or special needs. Policies and practices must explicitly address accessibility issues, ensuring that digital resources and tools are designed to accommodate diverse learning styles and abilities. Initiatives such as India's mobile education vans, which bring technology-enabled learning to underserved populations, exemplify the commitment to equity and inclusion in the digital education landscape (Digital India, 2022).

Strategies for Enhancing Accessibility:

- **Universal Design for Learning (UDL):** Implement UDL principles to develop educational technologies that can accommodate different learning styles and abilities.

- **Infrastructure Development:** Ensure that all students, especially those from underserved communities, have access to necessary technological infrastructure, including high-speed internet and digital devices.

Probabilistic Analysis for Accessibility Improvement:

- **Prior Probability (P):** Assume the initial belief in the success of accessibility initiatives is P(Accessibility Success) = 0.60 (60%).

- **Likelihood (L):** Given new initiatives like mobile education vans, the probability of successful accessibility improvement is P(Success | New Initiatives) = 0.80 (80%).

Calculate the total probability of accessibility success:

- **P(Success):** Assume the probability of success without new initiatives is P(Success | No New Initiatives) = 0.30 (30%).
- **Total Probability Calculation:**
  - P(Success) = (P(Success | New Initiatives) * P(Accessibility Success)) + (P(Success | No New Initiatives) * (1 - P(Accessibility Success)))
  - P(Success) = (0.80 * 0.60) + (0.30 * 0.40) = 0.48 + 0.12 = 0.60

Update the belief in the success of accessibility initiatives after observing positive outcomes:

- **Posterior Probability (P'):**
  - P'(Accessibility Success | Success) = (P(Success | New Initiatives) * P(Accessibility Success)) / P(Success)
  - P'(Accessibility Success | Success) = (0.80 * 0.60) / 0.60 = 0.80

This updated belief of 80% indicates a strong confidence level in the effectiveness of accessibility initiatives following the implementation of new strategies like mobile education vans.

Challenges and Solutions for Technology Integration in Education

Implementing technology in educational settings presents a complex array of
challenges. This section examines these challenges in detail, providing comprehensive solutions and citing examples from successful implementations to
ensure a deeper understanding of effective strategies in overcoming potential
obstacles. The implementation of technology in educational settings presents a
complex array of challenges that require comprehensive and nuanced solutions.
This section examines these challenges in detail, providing in-depth analysis
of potential solutions and citing examples from successful implementations to
ensure a deeper understanding of effective strategies in overcoming potential
obstacles.

One of the primary barriers to technology integration in education is the lack of
necessary infrastructure, including insufficient internet access and inadequate
digital devices, particularly in underprivileged and rural areas. This digital
divide not only limits access to educational resources but also creates disparities
in the quality of education received by students in different regions. To address
this issue, substantial investment in infrastructure is required, often necessitating collaboration between government entities, private sector companies, and
educational institutions. The 'ConnectED' program in the United States serves
as a model for such initiatives, aiming to connect 99% of students to high-speed
internet. This ambitious program involves partnerships between the government
and private companies to fund and facilitate the expansion of digital access
(Federal Communications Commission, 2021).

The implementation of such large-scale infrastructure projects requires careful
planning and coordination. For instance, in rural areas, solutions may include
the deployment of satellite internet or mobile broadband technologies to overcome geographical barriers. In urban areas with existing infrastructure, efforts
might focus on upgrading and expanding network capacity to handle increased
data traffic from educational applications. Moreover, the provision of digital
devices to students is a critical component of addressing accessibility challenges.
Programs like Uruguay's Plan Ceibal, which provides a laptop to every primary
school student in the country, demonstrate the potential of nationwide device
distribution initiatives (Plan Ceibal, 2020). However, such programs must also
consider device maintenance, replacement cycles, and technical support to ensure
long-term sustainability. Many educators lack the necessary training to integrate
technology effectively in their teaching practices, which can significantly hinder
the adoption and effective use of digital tools. This challenge is particularly acute
in regions where technology adoption in education is relatively recent or where
there is a significant age gap between teachers and the digital-native students
they instruct. Developing comprehensive and ongoing professional development
programs is crucial to address this challenge. The Singapore Ministry of Education's 'ICT Masterplans' provide an excellent example of a structured approach

to enhancing teachers' ICT skills. These plans focus on building teachers' competencies through a combination of formal training programs, workshops, and peer-learning opportunities (Ministry of Education, Singapore, 2021). Finland's approach to teacher training in technology integration serves as another noteworthy example. The country's emphasis on embedding digital skills within teacher education programs ensures that new teachers enter the profession with a strong foundation in educational technology (Finnish National Agency for Education, 2020).

Traditional teaching methods may not align well with new technological tools, requiring significant pedagogical adjustments. This misalignment can lead to ineffective use of technology, where digital tools are merely substituted for traditional methods without leveraging their full potential to transform learning experiences. To address this challenge, schools can adopt blended learning models that combine traditional teaching with technology-based instruction to gradually integrate new methods. The Flipped Classroom model, for instance, where students learn new content online by watching video lectures at home and use classroom time for more interactive activities, has proven effective in various contexts (Bergmann & Sams, 2012). The Success Academy Charter Schools network in New York provides an example of effective pedagogical adjustment. Their blended learning approach combines teacher-led instruction with adaptive learning software, allowing for personalized learning paths for each student (Success Academy, 2022).

There is a significant risk that technology-enhanced education could widen the achievement gap between students from different socio-economic backgrounds due to varying access to technology. This digital divide extends beyond mere access to devices and internet connectivity; it also encompasses disparities in digital literacy and the quality of technology-enhanced learning experiences. Implementing policies that specifically target equity and inclusion is essential to address this challenge. Providing subsidized or free devices and internet access to low-income families can help level the playing field. Programs like LAUSD's iPad initiative, which aims to provide free tablets to every student, demonstrate a commitment to inclusivity (Los Angeles Times, 2014). The state of Maine's learning technology initiative serves as a model for promoting equity in educational technology. The program not only provides laptops to all middle school students but also includes comprehensive teacher training and technical support to ensure effective use (Maine Department of Education, 2022).

The increased use of digital tools in education raises significant concerns about data privacy and security, particularly for minors. The collection and storage of student data, including personal information, academic records, and online behaviors, creates potential vulnerabilities that must be carefully managed. Establishing robust data protection regulations and ensuring that all educational technologies comply with these standards is crucial. The General Data Protection Regulation (GDPR) in the European Union provides a strong framework for protecting personal data, including specific provisions for children's data (EU

GDPR, 2018). The U.S. Department of Education's Privacy Technical Assistance Center offers resources and guidance for educational institutions on protecting student privacy in the digital age (U.S. Department of Education, 2022).

Measuring the impact of technology on educational outcomes can be complex and requires sophisticated assessment tools. Traditional assessment methods may not adequately capture the nuanced effects of technology integration on learning processes and outcomes. Developing comprehensive evaluation frameworks that incorporate both qualitative and quantitative methods can provide more nuanced insights into the effectiveness of technology integration. The OECD's PISA assessments, for instance, have begun to include digital literacy components to better assess the impact of technology in education (OECD, 2021). The AltSchool network in the United States provides an example of innovative approaches to evaluation in technology-rich learning environments. Their personalized learning platform incorporates continuous assessment and feedback loops to inform instructional decisions and track student progress (AltSchool, 2022).

KEY OBSERVATIONS:

Infrastructure and Accessibility Challenges

Challenge: One of the primary barriers to technology integration in education is the lack of necessary infrastructure, including insufficient internet access and inadequate digital devices, particularly in underprivileged and rural areas.

Solution: To address this issue, substantial investment in infrastructure is required. Initiatives like the 'ConnectED' program in the United States, which aims to connect 99% of students to high-speed internet, serve as a model. This program involves partnerships between the government and private companies to fund and facilitate the expansion of digital access (Federal Communications Commission, 2021).

Teacher Training and Technological Proficiency

Challenge: Many educators lack the necessary training to integrate technology effectively in their teaching practices, which can hinder the adoption of digital tools.

Solution: Developing comprehensive professional development programs is crucial. For example, the Singapore Ministry of Education's 'ICT Masterplans' focus on enhancing teachers' ICT skills through structured training programs and workshops (Ministry of Education, Singapore, 2021). These programs are designed to be ongoing and evolving, ensuring that teachers' skills remain up-to-date as new technologies emerge.

Pedagogical Adjustment to Technology

Challenge: Traditional teaching methods may not align well with new technological tools, requiring significant pedagogical adjustments.

Solution: Schools can adopt blended learning models that combine traditional teaching with technology-based instruction to gradually integrate new methods. The Flipped Classroom model, for instance, where students learn new content online by watching video lectures at home and use classroom time for more interactive activities, has proven effective in various contexts (Bergmann & Sams, 2012).

Equity and Inclusivity Concerns

Challenge: There is a risk that technology-enhanced education could widen the achievement gap between students from different socio-economic backgrounds due to varying access to technology.

Solution: Implementing policies that specifically target equity and inclusion is essential. For example, providing subsidized or free devices and internet access to low-income families can help level the playing field. Programs like LAUSD's iPad initiative, which aims to provide free tablets to every student, demonstrate a commitment to inclusivity (Los Angeles Times, 2014).

Data Privacy and Security Issues

Challenge: Increased use of digital tools raises concerns about data privacy and security, particularly for minors.

Solution: Establishing robust data protection regulations and ensuring that all educational technologies comply with these standards is crucial. The General Data Protection Regulation (GDPR) in the European Union provides a strong framework for protecting personal data, including specific provisions for children's data (EU GDPR, 2018).

Evaluation and Continuous Improvement

Challenge: Measuring the impact of technology on educational outcomes can be complex and requires sophisticated assessment tools.

Solution: Developing comprehensive evaluation frameworks that incorporate both qualitative and quantitative methods can provide more nuanced insights into the effectiveness of technology integration. For instance, the OECD's PISA assessments have begun to include digital literacy components to better assess the impact of technology in education (OECD, 2021).

Future Directions in Educational Technology

As educational systems continue to evolve, anticipating and planning for future technological advancements is crucial. This section explores potential future directions in educational technology, identifying emerging trends and technologies that could significantly impact teaching and learning. As educational systems increasingly integrate technology, evaluating its impact on educational outcomes becomes crucial. This section discusses methodologies and approaches for assessing the effectiveness of technology in education, focusing on key metrics, tools, and studies that illustrate the diverse impacts of technology on learning. Designing effective evaluation frameworks is essential for measuring the impact of technology in education accurately.

These frameworks should include both qualitative and quantitative measures to assess a range of outcomes, including student engagement, academic achievement, and skill development. The OECD's Centre for Educational Research and Innovation advocates for mixed-methods approaches that combine student performance data, teacher feedback, and classroom observations to evaluate the impact of technology-enhanced learning environments (OECD, 2021). This approach allows for a holistic view of how technology affects various aspects of education, providing a comprehensive understanding of its effectiveness and areas for improvement. Data analytics and learning analytics have emerged as powerful tools for assessing educational outcomes. By analyzing data generated from students' interactions with digital tools, educators can gain insights into learning behaviors, proficiency levels, and the effectiveness of different teaching methods. Platforms like Knewton exemplify this approach, providing adaptive learning experiences that track student progress and adapt in real-time to their needs. By analyzing this data, educators can identify patterns and make informed decisions to improve instructional strategies and student outcomes (Knewton, 2022). This data-driven approach enables a more personalized and responsive educational experience, potentially leading to improved learning outcomes. Conducting detailed case studies on specific instances of technology integration can provide deep insights into its effectiveness and the conditions that contribute to its success or failure. For example, a study conducted on the use of iPads in a Californian school district explored the devices' impact on student literacy development. The study found that with proper support and strategic use, iPads significantly enhanced students' reading abilities by providing interactive and engaging learning materials (California Education Department, 2021). Such case studies offer valuable insights into the practical implementation of educational technology and its effects on specific learning outcomes.

Longitudinal studies that track students over time are crucial for understanding the sustainability and lasting effects of tech-based interventions. These studies help determine the long-term impacts of technology on education, providing a more comprehensive view of its effectiveness beyond short-term gains. Harvard University's Graduate School of Education is conducting a five-year study on the effects of virtual reality (VR) learning environments on high school students' understanding of complex scientific concepts. The ongoing study aims to measure changes in conceptual understanding and interest in STEM subjects (Harvard Education, 2021). Such longitudinal research is essential for informing long-term educational technology strategies and policies. Implementing continuous feedback mechanisms that allow students and teachers to report their experiences and outcomes with educational technology is vital for ongoing evaluation and improvement. These mechanisms provide real-time insights into the usability and effectiveness of technological tools in the classroom. Singapore's Ministry of Education exemplifies this approach by utilizing a digital feedback tool that enables teachers and students to provide immediate feedback on digital tools and content.

This real-time feedback is used to make iterative improvements to digital learning resources (Ministry of Education, Singapore, 2022). Such feedback loops ensure that educational technology remains relevant, user-friendly, and aligned with the needs of both educators and learners. The evaluation of technology's impact on educational outcomes requires a multi-faceted approach that combines rigorous research methodologies with practical, real-world assessments. By employing a combination of evaluation frameworks, data analytics, case studies, longitudinal research, and continuous feedback mechanisms, educators and policymakers can gain a comprehensive understanding of how technology affects learning. This holistic approach to evaluation not only helps in assessing the current effectiveness of educational technology but also informs future developments and improvements in the field. As technology continues to evolve and integrate further into educational systems, robust evaluation methods will remain crucial in ensuring that these innovations genuinely enhance learning experiences and outcomes for all students.

KEY OBSERVATIONS:

Integration of Artificial Intelligence

Future Trend: Artificial Intelligence (AI) is poised to revolutionize educational environments by providing personalized learning experiences at scale. AI can automate administrative tasks, offer personalized tutoring, and adapt resources to meet the learning needs of individual students.

Strategic Implementation: Schools and educational institutions should consider partnerships with AI development companies to create and implement AI tools that are specifically designed for educational use. For example, the use of AI-driven analytics platforms like IBM's Watson Education, which provides insights into learning patterns and helps tailor content accordingly, can enhance instructional effectiveness and student engagement (IBM, 2022).

Augmented and Virtual Reality (AR/VR)

Future Trend: AR and VR technologies offer immersive learning experiences that can transform the traditional classroom setting. These technologies can bring abstract concepts to life, making learning more engaging and accessible, especially in fields like science, history, and art.

Strategic Implementation: Incorporating AR and VR into curricula requires not only investment in technology but also in content development. Educational systems should work with content developers to create immersive and interactive learning modules. An example is Google's Expeditions app, which allows students to explore different environments and historical sites through VR (Google, 2021).

Blockchain in Education

Future Trend: Blockchain technology has potential applications in education, particularly in verifying qualifications and managing student records securely. This technology ensures that educational credentials are tamper-proof and easily verifiable, facilitating greater mobility and transparency for students worldwide.

Strategic Implementation: Educational institutions should explore blockchain for certificate issuance and record keeping. Initiatives like the MIT Media Lab's Digital Certificates Project, which issues blockchain-based certifications, demonstrate how this technology can be used to securely issue and store educational credentials (MIT Media Lab, 2021).

Internet of Things (IoT) in Smart Educational Environments

Future Trend: IoT can transform educational facilities into smart environments that enhance learning, safety, and energy efficiency. Sensors and connected devices can automate many aspects of classroom management, from attendance tracking to environmental control, creating more conducive learning environments.

Strategic Implementation: Schools should begin by implementing pilot projects in IoT integration, focusing on areas like energy management and security to demonstrate the benefits and feasibility of smart classrooms. For instance, the University of California's Smart Campus initiative uses IoT to optimize energy use and improve campus safety (University of California, 2021).

Lifelong and Ubiquitous Learning

Future Trend: Technology enables lifelong learning opportunities outside traditional classroom settings. Mobile learning platforms and microlearning modules allow individuals to learn at their own pace and integrate education into their daily lives, catering to continuous professional development and personal growth.

Strategic Implementation: Educational systems should support and promote the development of mobile learning applications and platforms that offer flexible, bite-sized learning opportunities. Platforms like Udemy and Coursera provide courses that users can access on their smartphones, allowing for learning on the go (Coursera, 2022).

Evaluating the Impact of Technology on Educational Outcomes

As educational systems increasingly integrate technology, evaluating its impact on educational outcomes becomes crucial. This section discusses methodologies and approaches for assessing the effectiveness of technology in education, focusing on key metrics, tools, and studies that illustrate the diverse impacts of technology on learning.

KEY OBSERVATIONS:

Designing Effective Evaluation Frameworks

Methodology: Establishing comprehensive evaluation frameworks is essential for measuring the impact of technology in education accurately. These frameworks should include both qualitative and quantitative measures to assess a range of outcomes, including student engagement, academic achievement, and skill development.

Implementation Example: The OECD's Centre for Educational Research and Innovation advocates for mixed-methods approaches that combine student performance data, teacher feedback, and classroom observations to evaluate the impact of technology-enhanced learning environments (OECD, 2021). This approach allows for a holistic view of how technology affects various aspects of education.

Utilizing Data Analytics and Learning Analytics

Methodology: Data analytics and learning analytics are powerful tools for assessing educational outcomes. By analyzing data generated from students' interactions with digital tools, educators can gain insights into learning behaviors, proficiency levels, and the effectiveness of different teaching methods.

Implementation Example: Platforms like Knewton provide adaptive learning experiences that track student progress and adapt in real-time to their needs. By analyzing this data, educators can identify patterns and make informed decisions to improve instructional strategies and student outcomes (Knewton, 2022).

Case Study Evaluations

Methodology: Conducting detailed case studies on specific instances of technology integration can provide deep insights into its effectiveness and the conditions that contribute to its success or failure.

Implementation Example: A study conducted on the use of iPads in a Californian school district explored the devices' impact on student literacy development. The study found that with proper support and strategic use, iPads significantly enhanced students' reading abilities by providing interactive and engaging learning materials (California Education Department, 2021).

Longitudinal Studies

Methodology: Longitudinal studies that track students over time can help determine the long-term impacts of technology on education. These studies are crucial for understanding the sustainability and lasting effects of tech-based interventions.

Implementation Example: Harvard University's Graduate School of Education is conducting a five-year study on the effects of virtual reality (VR) learning environments on high school students' understanding of complex scientific concepts. The ongoing study aims to measure changes in conceptual understanding and interest in STEM subjects (Harvard Education, 2021).

Feedback Mechanisms and Continuous Improvement

Methodology: Implementing continuous feedback mechanisms that allow students and teachers to report their experiences and outcomes with educational technology is vital for ongoing evaluation and improvement.

Implementation Example: Singapore's Ministry of Education utilizes a digital feedback tool that allows teachers and students to provide immediate feedback on the usability and effectiveness of digital tools and content. This real-time feedback is used to make iterative improvements to digital learning resources (Ministry of Education, Singapore, 2022).

Scalability and Sustainability of Technological Solutions in Education

As educational technology continues to evolve, addressing the scalability and sustainability of these innovations is paramount. This section explores the challenges and strategies associated with scaling educational technology initiatives and maintaining their effectiveness and efficiency over time. The scalability and sustainability of technological solutions in education present complex challenges that require nuanced strategies and long-term planning. These issues are particularly crucial as educational systems worldwide seek to leverage technology for improved learning outcomes while grappling with resource constraints and rapid technological change.

The scalability and sustainability of technological solutions in education present complex challenges that require nuanced strategies and long-term planning. These issues are particularly crucial as educational systems worldwide seek to leverage technology for improved learning outcomes while grappling with resource constraints and rapid technological change. Addressing the scalability and sustainability of educational technology requires a multifaceted approach that considers infrastructural, pedagogical, and economic factors.

Scalability challenges in educational technology are multifaceted, encompassing infrastructural, pedagogical, and socioeconomic dimensions. The variability in regional infrastructure poses a significant barrier to uniform implementation of technology-based learning solutions. For instance, while urban areas may benefit from high-speed internet and advanced digital infrastructure, rural and remote regions often struggle with basic connectivity. This digital divide is not merely a matter of access but also impacts the quality and consistency of educational experiences. In India, for example, the Digital India initiative has made strides in bringing internet connectivity to rural areas, but challenges persist in ensuring stable connections and adequate bandwidth for interactive learning platforms. The disparity in digital literacy levels between urban and rural populations further complicates the scalability of educational technology solutions, necessitating tailored approaches that consider these varied contexts.

Differing educational standards across regions and countries present another scalability challenge. Educational technology solutions that align with the curriculum and pedagogical approaches of one region may not seamlessly translate to another. This issue is particularly pronounced in countries with decentralized education systems, where state or provincial standards may vary significantly. The United States, for instance, faces this challenge with its state-led education policies, making it difficult to implement nationwide educational technology initiatives without substantial customization. Addressing this requires flexible technological solutions that can be adapted to diverse educational standards while maintaining core functionality and effectiveness.

Resource limitations, both financial and human, pose significant barriers to scaling educational technology. The initial investment in hardware, software, and infrastructure can be substantial, particularly for comprehensive, system-wide implementations. Ongoing costs for maintenance, upgrades, and professional development further strain educational budgets. The One Laptop per Child (OLPC) initiative, while ambitious in its goals, faced challenges in scaling due to the high costs associated with providing and maintaining laptops in resource-constrained environments. This underscores the need for sustainable funding models and cost-effective technological solutions that can be realistically implemented and maintained over time.

Ensuring the sustainability of educational technology initiatives is equally challenging. Technological obsolescence is a persistent concern, with hardware and software rapidly becoming outdated in the face of continuous technological advancements. This necessitates regular updates and replacements, which can be costly and logistically complex, especially for large-scale implementations. The Los Angeles Unified School District's iPad initiative, launched in 2013, illustrates the challenges of sustainability. The program faced issues with outdated software, incompatibility with standardized testing requirements, and the need for frequent device replacements, ultimately leading to its discontinuation.

The need for continuous professional development presents another sustainability challenge. As educational technology evolves, educators must continuously update their skills to effectively integrate new tools and methodologies into their teaching practices. This requires ongoing investment in training programs and support systems, which can be resource-intensive. Finland's approach to educational technology integration offers a model for addressing this challenge. The country's national education technology strategy includes substantial investment in teacher training, recognizing that the effectiveness of technological tools is largely dependent on the ability of educators to use them effectively.

Effective integration practices that support both scalability and sustainability are crucial. This involves establishing robust IT support systems that can manage and maintain technological infrastructure across diverse educational settings. Regular updates to educational content and technology are essential to ensure relevance and effectiveness over time. Strategic funding models that account for both initial implementation and long-term maintenance are necessary for sustainable integration. South Korea's SMART Education initiative exemplifies a comprehensive approach to scalable and sustainable technology integration. The program includes nationwide implementation of digital textbooks and online resources, supported by the country's advanced digital infrastructure and sustained government funding.

Long-term impact assessments are vital for understanding the true effectiveness of educational technology initiatives. These assessments should go beyond short-term metrics to evaluate educational outcomes, technology adoption rates, and return on investment over extended periods. The University of California system's longitudinal study of its integrated digital education platforms provides valuable insights into the long-term impact of technology integration in higher education. Such studies are essential for informing future policy decisions and refining implementation strategies.

Successful models from around the world demonstrate the importance of context-specific solutions, sustained investment in infrastructure and professional development, and ongoing evaluation and adaptation. As educational systems continue to navigate the complex landscape of technological integration, these considerations will be crucial in ensuring that the benefits of educational technology are realized equitably and sustainably across diverse educational contexts. The scalability and sustainability of technological solutions in education remain ongoing challenges that require continuous attention and innovation to overcome.

KEY OBSERVATIONS:

Challenges to Scalability

Challenges: Scaling technology solutions in education can encounter several barriers, including variability in regional infrastructure, differing educational standards, and resource limitations. These factors can affect the uniform implementation and effectiveness of technology-based learning across diverse educational environments.

Strategic Considerations: Understanding local contexts and tailoring technological implementations accordingly is crucial. For example, the variation in internet connectivity and digital literacy levels across urban and rural areas requires adaptable solutions that consider these disparities (UNESCO, 2021).

Ensuring Sustainability

Challenges: Sustainability issues often stem from ongoing costs, technological obsolescence, and the need for continuous professional development. Ensuring that technological interventions remain relevant and financially viable over time is a significant concern for educational institutions.

Strategic Considerations: Developing partnerships with technology providers that include support and updates can mitigate the risk of obsolescence. Additionally, adopting open-source technologies and community-driven content can reduce costs and enhance sustainability (Open Source Initiative, 2021).

Effective Integration Practices

Methodology: Effective integration of technology into educational systems requires practices that support both scalability and sustainability. This includes the establishment of robust IT support systems, regular updates to educational content and technology, and strategic funding models that ensure long-term viability.

Implementation Example: Finland's national education technology strategy includes significant investment in teacher training, infrastructure, and partnerships with tech companies to ensure that technology integration is both scalable and sustainable (Finnish National Agency for Education, 2022).

Case Study: Scalable Models from Around the World

Case Study 1: South Korea's SMART Education Initiative: South Korea's SMART (Strategy for Massive Access to Resources in Technology) Education initiative showcases a scalable model where digital textbooks, online resources, and connected classrooms are implemented nationwide, supported by the country's high internet connectivity rates and government funding (Korean Ministry of Education, 2021).

Case Study 2: Rwanda's One Laptop per Child Program: This program is an example of adapting technology solutions to less developed infrastructure. The initiative focuses on providing laptops to children and includes solar-powered solutions for areas without reliable electricity (One Laptop per Child Association, 2021).

Long-Term Impact Assessments

Methodology: To truly understand the impact of scalability and sustainability efforts, long-term impact assessments are essential. These assessments should measure educational outcomes, technology adoption rates, and return on investment over extended periods.

Implementation Example: The longitudinal study conducted by the University of California system evaluates the impact of its integrated digital education platforms over a decade, providing insights into the effectiveness and sustainability of its tech-based initiatives (University of California, 2021).

Recommendations for Technology Integration in Education

Integrating technology into educational systems involves not only the deployment of tools and resources but also the formulation of supportive policies that encourage effective use and sustainable development. This section outlines key policy implications and provides recommendations to ensure that technology integration is efficient, equitable, and beneficial to all stakeholders in the educational landscape. The integration of technology in education necessitates comprehensive policy frameworks to ensure effective, equitable, and sustainable implementation. These policies must address a range of issues, from funding and access to data privacy and professional development, creating an environment that fosters the judicious use of technology in educational settings. Governments play a crucial role in establishing clear, comprehensive policies that delineate responsibilities across all levels of the educational system. Sweden's national digital strategy for schools exemplifies this approach, providing specific goals for technology use in education, supported by government funding and guidelines. This model demonstrates how well-crafted policies can create a cohesive framework for technology integration, ensuring alignment between educational objectives and technological implementation. A primary concern in technology integration is the potential to exacerbate existing educational inequalities. Policies must explicitly address equity and access issues to prevent the digital divide from becoming an insurmountable barrier to learning. Programs like the U.S. Federal Communications Commission's E-Rate initiative, which offers discounts to schools and libraries for telecommunications and internet access, serve as valuable models for promoting equitable access to educational technology. Such policies are essential in ensuring that technology serves as a bridge rather than a divider in educational attainment. The rapid evolution of educational technology necessitates ongoing professional development for educators. Policies should mandate and support continuous training programs embedded within the school calendar, focusing on both pedagogical and technical skills required for effective technology integration. These programs should be dynamic, adapting to emerging technologies and pedagogical approaches, ensuring that educators remain at the forefront of educational innovation. By prioritizing professional development, policies can ensure that the potential of educational technology is fully realized in the classroom, benefiting both teachers and students.

Public-private partnerships present a valuable avenue for addressing the challenges posed by the rapid pace of technological change in education. Policies should encourage collaboration between educational institutions and the private sector, leveraging industry expertise and resources to develop and implement innovative educational technologies. Singapore's FutureSchools@Singapore program exemplifies this approach, fostering collaboration between the Ministry of Education and industry leaders to advance innovative teaching practices and digital resources. Such partnerships can accelerate the development and adoption of cutting-edge educational technologies, keeping public education systems

competitive and relevant in a fast-changing technological landscape. As the
use of technology in education increases, so does the importance of robust data
governance and privacy standards. Policies must establish stringent guidelines
for data collection, storage, and sharing, aligning with international standards
such as the European Union's General Data Protection Regulation (GDPR).
These policies should prioritize the protection of student privacy and personal
information, ensuring that the benefits of educational technology do not come
at the cost of individual rights and data security. Clear, enforceable data governance policies are essential in building trust among stakeholders and ensuring
the responsible use of technology in educational settings. As such, policies should
mandate continuous evaluation and adaptation of educational technology initiatives. Regular assessment of the impact of technology on educational outcomes is
crucial to ensure that investments yield positive results and that implementation
strategies remain effective. The establishment of independent review bodies,
such as the proposed Educational Technology Agency in the UK, can provide
valuable oversight and facilitate the sharing of best practices across educational
institutions. By embedding evaluation and adaptation mechanisms in policy
frameworks, educational systems can remain responsive to technological advancements and evolving pedagogical needs, ensuring that technology integration
continues to enhance learning outcomes effectively.

Development of Comprehensive Technology Policies

Policy Need: Educational technology policies should encompass aspects such
as funding, access, training, and data privacy to create an environment that
fosters effective technology use in schools.

Recommendation: Governments should establish clear, comprehensive policies
that define roles and responsibilities at all levels — from school administrators
to teachers to IT staff. An example of effective policy development is Sweden's
national digital strategy for schools, which includes specific goals for technology
use in education, supported by government funding and guidelines (Swedish
Ministry of Education, 2021).

Enhancing Equity and Access

Policy Need: Technology should bridge educational gaps rather than widen
them. Policies must address issues of equity and access to prevent the digital
divide from becoming a barrier to learning.

Recommendation: Implement policies that ensure all students have access to
necessary technology and internet connectivity. Programs like the U.S. Federal
Communications Commission's E-Rate program, which provides discounts to
help schools and libraries obtain affordable telecommunications and internet
access, can serve as a model (Federal Communications Commission, 2021).

Supporting Educator Professional Development

Policy Need: As educational technology evolves, continuous professional development for educators is crucial for them to remain effective in their roles.

Recommendation: Establish ongoing training programs that are embedded within the school calendar and supported by policy at the district or national level. These programs should focus on both the pedagogical and technical skills required to integrate technology effectively in the classroom.

Encouraging Public-Private Partnerships

Policy Need: The rapid pace of technological change can challenge public educational systems' ability to keep up without significant investment and innovation.

Recommendation: Foster public-private partnerships to leverage the expertise, resources, and innovation of the private sector in developing and implementing educational technologies. Successful partnerships can be seen in programs like Singapore's FutureSchools@Singapore, which involves collaboration between the Ministry of Education and industry leaders to develop innovative teaching practices and digital resources (Ministry of Education, Singapore, 2022).

Implementing Data Governance and Privacy Standards

Policy Need: With the increased use of technology comes the need to protect student data and ensure privacy.

Recommendation: Develop stringent data governance policies that comply with international standards such as the GDPR in the European Union. These policies should provide clear guidelines on data collection, storage, and sharing to protect students' privacy and personal information (European Commission, 2021).

Evaluation and Adaptation of Educational Technology

Policy Need: Continuous evaluation of the impact of technology on educational outcomes is necessary to ensure that investments are yielding positive results.

Recommendation: Policies should mandate regular evaluation and reporting on the effectiveness of technology in schools. This could involve setting up independent review bodies similar to the Educational Technology Agency proposed in the UK, which aims to assess the impact of educational technologies and share best practices (UK Department for Education, 2021).

Technological Trends and the Future in Education

This section examines emerging technological trends in education, focusing on Artificial Intelligence (AI), Virtual Reality (VR), Augmented Reality (AR), and blockchain technology. These innovations present significant potential for enhancing educational processes and outcomes, while also introducing new challenges and considerations. the integration of AI, VR, AR, and blockchain technologies in education offers exciting possibilities for enhancing learning experiences and outcomes. However, realizing this potential requires careful navigation of a complex set of technological, pedagogical, ethical, and societal challenges. As these technologies continue to evolve, ongoing research and long-term impact assessments will be crucial to refine implementation strategies and ensure that technological advancements genuinely serve to improve educational outcomes for all learners (Taylor et al., 2022). The future of education lies not in technology alone, but in the thoughtful integration of these tools within a broader ecosystem of effective pedagogical practices and equitable access to learning opportunities.

The landscape of education is undergoing a significant transformation driven by emerging technologies. This section examines the interplay between Artificial Intelligence (AI), Virtual Reality (VR), Augmented Reality (AR), and blockchain technology in shaping the future of education. These technologies, while distinct, are increasingly converging to create novel educational paradigms that challenge traditional teaching and learning methods. Artificial Intelligence stands at the forefront of this technological revolution in education. Its potential extends beyond mere automation of administrative tasks, delving into the realm of personalized learning experiences. AI's capacity to analyze vast amounts of data allows for the creation of adaptive learning systems that tailor educational content to individual student needs. For instance, intelligent tutoring systems can identify knowledge gaps and provide targeted instruction, potentially accelerating learning outcomes (Johnson et al., 2019).

However, the integration of AI in education is not without controversy. The use of AI-driven systems raises significant concerns about data privacy and the potential for algorithmic bias. As Brown and Lee (2021) argue, there is a pressing need to ensure that AI systems in education are transparent and built using diverse datasets to mitigate the risk of perpetuating or exacerbating existing inequalities. This challenge is particularly evident in the context of standardized testing and admissions processes, where AI-based decision-making could have far-reaching consequences on students' educational trajectories. The concerns surrounding AI in education are further complicated when considered alongside the immersive technologies of Virtual and Augmented Reality. While VR and AR offer unprecedented opportunities for experiential learning, their integration with AI systems raises new questions about the nature of assessment and the role of human educators. For example, VR simulations enhanced by AI could provide highly realistic and adaptive learning environments, but they also pose challenges in terms of how to evaluate student performance and ensure equitable access to these technologies (Williams, 2018). VR and AR technologies are redefining the boundaries of the traditional classroom, offering immersive experiences that were previously impossible or impractical. These technologies have shown particular promise in fields requiring spatial understanding or hands-on experience, such as architecture, medicine, and the natural sciences (Chen & Wang, 2020). However, the widespread adoption of VR and AR in education faces significant hurdles, including high equipment costs and the need for robust technical infrastructure. These barriers are particularly pronounced in under-resourced schools, potentially exacerbating existing educational inequalities (Garcia, 2019).

The integration of AI with VR and AR technologies presents both opportunities and challenges for addressing diverse learning needs. While these technologies offer unique opportunities for students with special educational needs by creating tailored, controlled environments (Thompson, 2021), they also raise questions about the potential for digital segregation. There is a risk that overreliance on technology-mediated instruction could reduce valuable face-to-face interactions, which are crucial for social and emotional development. As these immersive and adaptive technologies reshape the learning experience, blockchain emerges as a potential solution to the challenge of credentialing and record-keeping in this new educational landscape. Blockchain technology offers a decentralized and tamper-proof method for recording educational achievements, which could revolutionize how credentials are verified and shared across institutions and borders (Miller, 2022). This is particularly relevant in the context of the increasing modularization of education and the rise of micro-credentials, which traditional credentialing systems struggle to accommodate. The potential of blockchain in education extends beyond mere record-keeping. When combined with AI and immersive technologies, blockchain could enable new forms of personalized and verifiable learning experiences. For instance, smart contracts built on blockchain platforms could automate the award of micro-credentials based on achievements in AI-driven VR learning environments. However, as Anderson and Patel (2021) note, the implementation of blockchain in education also raises questions about data ownership, privacy, and the standardization of credentialing across diverse educational systems.

The convergence of these technologies – AI, VR, AR, and blockchain – presents a vision of education that is highly personalized, immersive, and transparently credentialed. However, realizing this vision requires addressing several key challenges. First and foremost is the issue of equity and access. As Roberts (2020) argues, there is a significant risk that the adoption of these technologies could widen the digital divide, further disadvantaging students from low-income backgrounds or under-resourced schools. Moreover, the effective integration of these technologies necessitates a fundamental rethinking of teacher training and professional development. As Johnson (2021) points out, educators need not only technical skills but also the pedagogical knowledge to effectively leverage these technologies in service of learning outcomes. This requires a significant investment in ongoing professional development and a reimagining of the role of the teacher in technology-rich learning environments. Ethical considerations also loom large in the discussion of these emerging technologies. Issues of data privacy, algorithmic bias, and the psychological impact of immersive technologies on developing minds must be carefully addressed (Smith & Brown, 2022). There is a need for robust policy frameworks to govern the use of these technologies in educational settings, balancing innovation with the protection of student rights and well-being.

Conclusion

Overview of Technological Integration in Education

This work has thoroughly examined the multifaceted impact of technology integration in education, highlighting its potential benefits, challenges, and implementation strategies across various contexts. The evidence suggests that while technology offers significant opportunities to enhance learning experiences and outcomes, its effective implementation requires a nuanced understanding of numerous factors. The study underscores the significant transformation brought about by integrating technology into educational systems. By examining the multifaceted impacts, we can see that technology has the potential to revolutionize learning environments, making them more adaptable, personalized, and effective. The integration of digital tools and platforms enables educators to offer a more interactive and engaging learning experience, fostering improved student outcomes and greater equity in education. However, the successful implementation of technology requires a deep understanding of the intricate interplay between various technical, pedagogical, and policy-related factors. These factors include the need for robust infrastructure, effective teacher training, and the development of supportive policies that address data privacy and equity issues. The potential benefits of technology in education are vast, but realizing these benefits necessitates a strategic and well-coordinated approach.

Personalized Learning and Global Connectivity

The analysis of personalized learning through AI and global connectivity reveals promising avenues for tailoring education to individual needs and fostering cross-cultural collaboration. Personalized learning technologies, powered by AI, allow for the customization of educational content to suit the unique learning styles and paces of individual students. Personalized learning technologies, powered by AI, represent one of the most promising advancements in modern education. These technologies allow for the customization of educational content to suit the unique learning styles and paces of individual students. Platforms such as Khan Academy and intelligent tutoring systems like Carnegie Learning's MATHia utilize sophisticated data analytics to provide a detailed understanding of a student's learning preferences, strengths, and areas for improvement. This tailored approach not only enhances student engagement but also improves comprehension and retention, leading to better academic outcomes. Global connectivity, facilitated by digital tools, further expands the horizons of education by breaking down geographical barriers and fostering cross-cultural collaboration. Video conferencing software, online forums, and virtual exchange programs enable students and educators from different parts of the world to collaborate on projects, share perspectives, and learn from one another. This global interaction not only enriches the educational experience but also prepares students for a more interconnected and diverse world. By exposing students to different cultures and viewpoints, global connectivity tools enhance critical thinking, empathy, and communication skills, which are essential for success in the 21st-century workforce.

Addressing Challenges: Digital Divide, Data Privacy, and Teacher Training

Significant challenges persist, particularly regarding the digital divide, data privacy, and the need for comprehensive teacher training. The digital divide remains a substantial barrier, with unequal access to technology and the internet preventing many students from benefiting from these advancements. Despite the promising potential of educational technology, significant challenges must be addressed to ensure its successful integration. One of the primary challenges is the digital divide, which refers to the gap between individuals who have easy access to the internet and digital devices and those who do not. This divide exacerbates existing educational inequalities, particularly in underprivileged and rural areas. Efforts to bridge this divide must include providing the necessary hardware and internet access, as well as training for teachers and students to use these technologies effectively. Initiatives like mobile education vans in rural India, which bring internet-enabled devices and educational resources to remote communities, offer innovative solutions to this challenge. Data privacy is another critical concern in the integration of technology in education. The increasing use of AI and other technologies involves the collection and analysis of vast amounts of personal data, raising issues about how this data is stored, used, and protected. Ensuring robust data privacy and security measures is paramount to maintaining trust and safeguarding students' rights. Educational institutions must implement comprehensive data governance policies that address these concerns and ensure the ethical use of data. The effectiveness of technology in education also depends heavily on the proficiency and preparedness of teachers. Many educators lack the necessary training to utilize digital tools effectively, which can limit the potential benefits of technology-enhanced learning environments. Comprehensive professional development programs are essential to equip teachers with the skills and knowledge required to integrate technology into their teaching practices. These programs should cover not only technical skills but also pedagogical strategies for using technology to enhance learning. By investing in teacher training, educational institutions can ensure that educators are well-prepared to leverage technology for the benefit of their students.

Case Studies of Successful Technology Integration

The integration of technology in education has been successfully demonstrated through various case studies from around the world. In Finland, the use of AI to personalize learning has significantly improved student engagement and performance. The AI system analyzes individual student learning patterns, providing tailored recommendations that help teachers identify students who need additional support and adjust their instructional strategies accordingly. This data-driven approach to education exemplifies how technology can facilitate personalized learning and improve educational outcomes. Singapore's Smart Learning Spaces leverage the Internet of Things (IoT) to create adaptable and responsive learning environments. These classrooms are equipped with sensors and smart devices that adjust lighting, temperature, and physical layouts to optimize learning for different activities and teaching styles. The integration of real-time feedback systems allows students to interact dynamically with educational content, while teachers can continuously monitor student engagement and comprehension. This innovative use of technology has fostered a more conducive and personalized learning environment, enhancing the overall educational experience. In rural India, mobile education vans equipped with computers, internet access, and educational technology tools travel to remote areas to provide children with access to digital learning resources. This initiative has significantly expanded educational outreach, enabling children in underserved areas to access the same educational opportunities as their urban counterparts. By overcoming geographical and socio-economic barriers, mobile education vans demonstrate the potential of mobile technology to democratize education and bridge the digital divide. In the United States, the Rocketship Public Schools network employs a blended learning model that combines online digital media with traditional classroom methods. This approach allows for personalized instruction, with students alternating between engaging with digital content and receiving in-person instruction from teachers. Research has shown that blended learning models can lead to significant improvements in test scores and student comprehension, particularly in subjects like math and reading. These case studies collectively illustrate the diverse ways in which educational technology can be harnessed to enhance learning experiences and outcomes.

Comprehensive Framework for Technology Integration

To fully harness the transformative potential of technology in education, a robust and adaptable framework is essential. This framework should encompass three interconnected pillars: infrastructure and accessibility, teacher training and professional development, and curriculum integration and pedagogical adaptation. Infrastructure development is the foundation of any successful technology integration initiative. This involves ensuring universal access to high-speed internet connectivity, providing adequate and up-to-date hardware, and procuring software solutions tailored to educational needs. Governments and educational institutions must prioritize substantial investments in building and maintaining this technological backbone. Additionally, the infrastructure must be designed for scalability and adaptability to accommodate future technological advancements. Cloud-based solutions, modular hardware upgrades, and customizable software platforms can ensure that technology can be expanded to reach a wider audience and seamlessly integrate new tools as they emerge. Teacher training and professional development are critical components of the framework. Continuous professional development programs should equip educators with the skills to effectively use educational technologies and integrate them into their teaching practices. These programs should cover technical proficiency, data literacy, and pedagogical strategies for digital and blended learning environments. By investing in teacher training, educational institutions can empower educators to become facilitators of technology-enhanced learning, fostering a culture of innovation and continuous improvement. Curriculum integration and pedagogical adaptation involve rethinking traditional teaching methods to incorporate technology in ways that enhance learning. This requires a fundamental shift from lecture-based models to more student-centered, active learning approaches. The curriculum should include digital literacy as a core competency, equipping students with the skills to evaluate information critically, collaborate online, and create digital content. Technological tools should be viewed as integral components of the learning process, with interactive simulations, virtual field trips, online collaboration platforms, and adaptive learning software being leveraged to create engaging and personalized learning experiences.

Implementation Strategies and Policy Recommendations

Implementing a technology-driven educational framework requires comprehensive strategies that align with policy recommendations to ensure sustainable and effective integration. Strategic planning involves engaging all stakeholders, including government bodies, educational institutions, technology providers, teachers, students, and parents, in the planning process. By integrating diverse perspectives and expertise, the solutions implemented can be tailored to meet the specific needs and constraints of each educational system. Governments play a pivotal role in fostering technology integration through the development of clear and comprehensive policies. These policies should encompass guidelines for data privacy, robust funding models, and strategic infrastructure development initiatives. Policies must explicitly address equity issues to prevent the exacerbation of the digital divide. Substantial and sustained investments are required to build and maintain the digital infrastructure necessary for modern learning environments. Additionally, policies should promote ongoing professional development for educators and provide incentives for schools that successfully implement technology programs. Holistic planning involves considering all aspects of technology integration, from infrastructure and training to curriculum development and assessment. Engaging stakeholders ensures that technology initiatives are well-supported and meet the needs of the community. Ongoing evaluation is essential to monitor the effectiveness of technology integration efforts, identify areas for improvement, and adapt strategies as needed. Feedback mechanisms that allow teachers and students to share their experiences and suggest improvements foster a culture of continuous improvement and ensure that technology remains aligned with pedagogical goals.

Emerging Technologies and Future Trends

The potential of emerging technologies like AI, VR/AR, and blockchain is vast, but their integration into education is complex and requires careful consideration. AI has the potential to revolutionize education by providing personalized learning experiences, automating administrative tasks, and supporting data-driven decision-making. However, its integration raises ethical concerns about data privacy, bias, and the role of human educators. Educators and policymakers must work together to address these concerns and develop guidelines for the ethical use of AI in education. VR/AR technologies offer immersive learning experiences that can enhance understanding and engagement, particularly in subjects like science and history. These technologies allow students to explore environments and interact with content in ways that are not possible with traditional methods. However, the high cost and technical requirements of VR/AR technologies present significant barriers to widespread adoption. Educational institutions must consider these factors and explore ways to make VR/AR more accessible to all students. Blockchain technology has the potential to transform administrative processes in education, such as credentialing and transcripts. Its secure and transparent record-keeping capabilities can enhance the management of academic records and assessments. However, its implementation requires significant investment and expertise. Policymakers and educational institutions must explore the potential applications of blockchain in education and develop strategies to overcome the challenges associated with its integration.

Evaluation Methodologies and Scalability Considerations

Effective evaluation methodologies are necessary to measure the impact of technology on learning outcomes accurately. This involves not only quantitative metrics like test scores but also qualitative assessments of student engagement, teacher satisfaction, and overall educational experience. Evaluation frameworks should include mechanisms for collecting feedback from all stakeholders, including students, teachers, administrators, parents, and community members. This feedback can identify areas for improvement and guide adjustments to technology infrastructure and educational programs. Scalability considerations are crucial to ensure that successful pilot projects can be expanded to benefit a larger population. This requires careful planning, sufficient resources, and ongoing support to maintain the quality and effectiveness of technology initiatives. Educational institutions must develop strategies for scaling successful programs, including providing additional training for teachers, investing in infrastructure, and ensuring equitable access to technology. By addressing scalability considerations, educational systems can maximize the benefits of technology integration and ensure that all students have access to high-quality learning experiences.

Policy Implications

Comprehensive Technology Policies The integration of technology in education demands a comprehensive set of policies that cover all aspects of the process, from infrastructure development to training, curriculum adaptation, and assessment. Effective technology policies should provide clear guidelines and support mechanisms to ensure that technology initiatives align with educational goals and priorities. These policies must be developed in a way that they are adaptable to the rapidly evolving technological landscape and responsive to the unique needs of different educational contexts. Infrastructure Development: One of the fundamental components of comprehensive technology policies is the development and maintenance of robust infrastructure. This includes ensuring universal access to high-speed internet connectivity, which is the backbone of any digital learning environment. Governments and educational institutions must invest in building and upgrading infrastructure to support digital learning. This includes not only internet connectivity but also the provision of adequate hardware, such as computers, tablets, and interactive whiteboards. Policies should mandate regular assessments and upgrades to the technological infrastructure to keep pace with advancements and ensure reliability and efficiency. Training and Professional Development: Comprehensive technology policies must include provisions for continuous training and professional development of educators. Teachers need to be proficient in using educational technologies and integrating them into their teaching practices effectively. Policies should support the development of training programs that cover a range of competencies, from basic digital literacy to advanced instructional technologies. These programs should be designed to be flexible and accessible, allowing teachers to learn at their own pace and apply their knowledge in practical settings. Additionally, policies should encourage the creation of professional learning communities where educators can share best practices and collaborate on innovative teaching methods. Curriculum Development and Pedagogical Adaptation: Policies should also address the integration of technology into the curriculum and pedagogical practices. This involves redesigning the curriculum to include digital literacy as a core competency, ensuring that students are equipped with the skills needed to navigate the digital world. Technological tools should be integrated into the curriculum not as supplementary materials but as fundamental components that enhance learning. Interactive simulations, virtual labs, and digital collaboration platforms can create more engaging and personalized learning experiences. Policies should support ongoing research and development in educational technologies to identify and implement the most effective tools and strategies. Assessment and Evaluation: The assessment methods must evolve to measure not only content knowledge but also the digital skills and competencies that students develop through technology-enhanced learning. Policies should promote the use of digital assessments that provide real-time feedback and adapt to the student's ability level. These assessments can offer a more accurate and comprehensive evaluation of student performance, helping educators identify areas for improvement and tailor their instruction accordingly. Additionally, policies should mandate regular evaluations of technology integration efforts to assess their impact on educational outcomes and ensure continuous improvement. Enhanced Equity Measures Equity in education is a critical issue, and technology integration must address the disparities that exist among different socio-economic groups. Enhanced equity measures are essential to ensure that all students, regardless of their socio-economic background, have access to the benefits of technology. Access to Devices and Internet: One of the primary equity measures is providing devices and internet access to underprivileged students. Many students from low-income families lack the necessary technology to participate in digital learning, which exacerbates educational inequalities. Policies should include initiatives to distribute devices, such as laptops and tablets, to students who cannot afford them. Additionally, providing affordable or free internet access to underprivileged families is crucial. Governments can collaborate with private sector partners to create programs that subsidize internet costs or establish community internet access points in underserved areas. Support for Disadvantaged Schools: Schools in disadvantaged areas often struggle with limited resources and outdated technology. Enhanced equity measures should include targeted support for these schools to ensure they have the necessary infrastructure and tools to provide quality education. This support can take the form of grants, funding for technology upgrades, and professional development programs for teachers. By investing in disadvantaged schools, policymakers can help bridge the gap between affluent and underprivileged communities and promote equal educational opportunities for all students. Inclusive Education: Equity measures should also focus on inclusive education, ensuring that students with disabilities have access to the necessary technologies and support. Assistive technologies, such as screen readers, speech-to-text software, and adaptive learning platforms, can help students with disabilities participate fully in digital learning environments. Policies should mandate the development and implementation of accessible digital content and tools that cater to the diverse needs of all students. Additionally, teacher training programs should include modules on inclusive education and the use of assistive technologies to support students with disabilities. Community Engagement and Partnerships: Engaging local communities and forming partnerships with various stakeholders is crucial for the success of equity measures. Community centers and libraries can serve as hubs for digital learning, providing access to technology and offering training sessions for students and parents. Policymakers should encourage collaborations between schools, local governments, non-profit organizations, and the private sector to create a supportive network that enhances access to educational technology. These partnerships can help mobilize resources, share expertise, and develop innovative solutions to address equity challenges. Strong Data Governance Standards With the increasing use of technology in education, the collection and analysis of personal data have become integral to improving learning outcomes. However, this also raises significant concerns about data privacy and security. Strong data governance standards are necessary to protect student privacy and ensure the ethical use of data in education. Data Collection and Storage: Policies should define clear guidelines for data collection and storage, specifying what data can be collected, how it should be stored, and who has access to it. These guidelines should prioritize the minimization of data collection, collecting only the information that is necessary for educational purposes. Data storage practices should include robust security measures, such as encryption and regular security audits, to protect against data breaches and unauthorized access. Additionally, policies should mandate the use of secure and compliant cloud storage solutions to ensure data integrity and availability. Data Usage and Sharing: The ethical use of data involves transparent policies on how data is used and shared. Educational institutions must inform students and parents about the types of data collected, the purposes for which it is used, and the entities with whom it is shared. Policies should prohibit the sale of student data to third parties and restrict data sharing to educational purposes only. Any sharing of data should be done with the explicit consent of students and parents, and the data should be anonymized to protect individual identities. Policies should also include provisions for regular audits and assessments to ensure compliance with data usage guidelines. Student Rights and Consent: Protecting student rights is a fundamental aspect of data governance. Policies should establish clear protocols for obtaining consent from students and parents before collecting and using their data. These protocols should be designed to ensure that consent is informed and voluntary. Students and parents should have the right to access their data, request corrections, and withdraw consent at any time. Additionally, policies should provide mechanisms for students and parents to file complaints and seek redress in cases of data misuse or breaches. Training and Awareness: To implement strong data governance standards, it is essential to raise awareness and provide training on data privacy and security. Educators, administrators, and staff must be trained on the principles of data protection and the specific policies and procedures in place. Training programs should cover topics such as data encryption, secure data handling, and recognizing potential security threats. Additionally, students and parents should be educated about their rights and responsibilities regarding data privacy. By fostering a culture of awareness and vigilance, educational institutions can enhance their data governance practices and build trust with stakeholders. Monitoring and Compliance: Effective data governance requires ongoing monitoring and compliance mechanisms to ensure adherence to policies and standards. Educational institutions should establish dedicated data protection officers or committees responsible for overseeing data governance practices. Regular audits and assessments should be conducted to identify vulnerabilities and areas for improvement. Policies should include clear consequences for non-compliance and establish protocols for responding to data breaches or violations. By maintaining rigorous monitoring and compliance measures, educational institutions can safeguard student data and uphold ethical standards.

Future Research Directions

Future research should focus on longitudinal studies of technology impact to understand the long-term effects on learning outcomes. These studies can provide valuable insights into the sustained benefits and potential drawbacks of technology integration, informing future policies and practices. Additionally, refining evaluation methodologies is necessary to develop more accurate and comprehensive tools for assessing the effectiveness of technology in education. This includes exploring new metrics and data sources, as well as incorporating qualitative assessments of student and teacher experiences.

The development of adaptive implementation strategies is also critical to ensure that technological innovations can be effectively integrated into diverse educational contexts. This involves designing flexible and scalable approaches that can be tailored to the specific needs and conditions of different schools and communities. By focusing on these areas, future research can contribute to the continuous improvement of technology-enhanced education and help educational systems navigate the complex landscape of technological change.

Final Thoughts

This work demonstrates that while technology has the potential to significantly enhance educational practices, its successful integration depends on addressing a complex array of technical, pedagogical, and policy-related challenges. By focusing on these areas, educational systems can leverage technology to create more engaging, effective, and inclusive learning environments. Preparing students for future challenges and opportunities in an increasingly interconnected and technologically advanced world requires a strategic and well-coordinated approach. This approach must include addressing the digital divide, ensuring data privacy, providing comprehensive teacher training, and developing robust policies to maximize the benefits of technology and foster a culture of innovation and continuous improvement.

The digital divide remains a significant barrier to the equitable integration of technology in education. This divide, characterized by disparities in access to digital devices and reliable internet connectivity, exacerbates existing educational inequalities, particularly in underprivileged and rural areas. To bridge this gap, policymakers must implement initiatives that provide necessary hardware and internet access to all students. This can include distributing laptops and tablets to students who cannot afford them and creating affordable or free internet access programs for low-income families. Additionally, innovative solutions like mobile education vans, which bring internet-enabled devices and educational resources to remote communities, can play a crucial role in ensuring that all students benefit from digital learning. By addressing these disparities, educational systems can create a more level playing field where every student has the opportunity to succeed in a digital age. Ensuring data privacy is another critical component of successful technology integration. The increasing use of AI and other technologies in education involves the collection and analysis of vast amounts of personal data, raising significant concerns about how this data is stored, used, and protected. Educational institutions must implement comprehensive data governance policies that prioritize the minimization of data collection, secure storage practices, and strict access controls. These policies should include clear guidelines on data usage and sharing, prohibiting the sale of student data to third parties and ensuring that any data sharing is done with explicit consent and for educational purposes only. By establishing robust data privacy measures, institutions can maintain trust and protect the rights of students. Comprehensive teacher training is essential for the effective use of technology in education. Many educators currently lack the necessary skills to utilize digital tools effectively, limiting the potential benefits of technology-enhanced learning environments.

Professional development programs should be designed to equip teachers with both the technical proficiency to use educational technologies and the pedagogical strategies to integrate them into their teaching practices. These training programs should cover a range of competencies, from basic digital literacy to advanced instructional technologies, and should be flexible and accessible to accommodate the diverse needs of educators. By investing in ongoing professional development, educational institutions can ensure that teachers are well-prepared to leverage technology to enhance student learning. Developing robust policies is crucial to supporting the integration of technology in education. These policies should address all aspects of technology integration, from infrastructure development and training to curriculum adaptation and assessment. Effective technology policies must provide clear guidelines and support mechanisms to ensure that technology initiatives align with educational goals and priorities. This includes investing in building and maintaining a reliable technological infrastructure, supporting continuous professional development for educators, and promoting the integration of digital literacy into the curriculum. Policies should also include provisions for regular evaluations of technology integration efforts to assess their impact on educational outcomes and identify areas for improvement. The ultimate goal of integrating technology in education is to create a system that not only enhances learning outcomes but also equips students with the skills and knowledge needed to thrive in the 21st century. This involves fostering a culture of innovation and continuous improvement, where technology is used to create more engaging, effective, and inclusive learning environments. By strategically addressing the digital divide, ensuring data privacy, providing comprehensive teacher training, and developing robust policies, educational institutions can maximize the benefits of technology. This strategic and well-coordinated approach will prepare students for future challenges and opportunities in an increasingly interconnected and technologically advanced world, ensuring that they are equipped with the critical thinking, creativity, and adaptability required for success in the global landscape.

References

Abbas, A., Smith, J., & Johnson, K. (2020). Structure-based singular value decomposition method. Journal of Water Resources, 45(2), 123-135.

Abid, M., Schneider, U. A., & Scheffran, J. (2017). Adaptation to climate change and its impacts on food productivity and household income: A case study of Pakistan. Climate Risk Management, 16, 123-144.

Abid, M., Schneider, U. A., & Scheffran, J. (2021). Evaluation of irrigation systems for increased efficiency. Journal of Agricultural Water Management, 23(1), 23-34.

Abhilash, P. C. (2021). Agricultural sustainability in the Indian subcontinent: A review. International Journal of Environmental Science and Technology, 18(4), 945-960.

Ahmed, A., Hameed, A., & Bukhari, S. (2020). Punjab Government's commitment towards environmental protection. Journal of Environmental Policy, 10(3), 211-230.

Akello, B. O. (2018). Barriers to sustainable agriculture adoption. Journal of Agricultural Extension and Rural Development, 10(4), 77-89.

Altieri, M. A., Funes-Monzote, F. R., & Petersen, P. (2015). Agroecologically efficient agricultural systems for smallholder farmers: Contributions to food sovereignty. Agronomy for Sustainable Development, 32(1), 1-13.

Aziz, J., Ahmed, S., & Khan, N. (2021). Pakistan's water resources management. Journal of Water Resources Planning and Management, 11(2), 98-112.

Baig, M. B., & Straquadine, G. S. (2011). Sustainable agriculture ensuring food security in Pakistan. Journal of Agriculture and Environment for International Development (JAEID), 105(3), 281-295.

Bastan, M., Javadizadeh, A., & Ahmadi, M. (2018). The impact of European Union agricultural policies on sustainable development. International Journal of Agricultural Economics, 34(3), 78-95.

Bergmann, J., & Sams, A. (2012). Flip Your Classroom: Reach Every Student in Every Class Every Day. International Society for Technology in Education.

Brown, J., & Smith, M. (1987). Definitions and key principles of sustainable agriculture. Journal of Sustainable Agriculture, 5(1), 45-56.

California Education Department. (2021). Impact of iPads on Student Literacy Development. California Education Department.

Carmela Annosi, M., Magnusson, M., & Martini, A. (2020). Technological innovation in agricultural systems. Journal of Innovation & Knowledge, 5(3), 123-136.

Charatsari, C., & Lioutas, E. D. (2019). Agroecological practices for sustainable farming. Journal of Agricultural and Environmental Ethics, 32(3), 431-446.

Chen, B., & Wang, Y. (2020). VR and AR in education: Potentials and challenges. Educational Technology & Society, 23(4), 12-25.

Christiaensen, L., Demery, L., & Kuhl, J. (2011). The role of agriculture in poverty reduction: An empirical perspective. World Development, 39(6), 847-860.

Coursera. (2022). Online Courses & Credentials From Top Educators. Coursera.

Coulibaly, P., Rodriguez, J. P., & Clark, L. (2021). FAO's definition and implementation of sustainable agriculture. Journal of Agricultural Science and Technology, 22(1), 12-23.

Digital India. (2022). Mobile Education Vans: Bridging the Education Gap in Rural India. Digital India.

Doe, J., & Smith, J. (2019). Inclusive education through technology. Journal of Special Education Technology, 34(2), 87-99.

EU GDPR. (2018). General Data Protection Regulation. European Commission.

Ebrahim, Z. (2019). Water management for equity in Punjab. Journal of Water Policy, 21(3), 234-245.

Federal Communications Commission. (2021). E-Rate: Universal Service Program for Schools and Libraries. FCC.

Finnish National Agency for Education. (2022). National Digital Strategy for Schools. Finnish National Agency for Education.

Global Education Conference. (2022). Global Education Conference Network. Global Education Conference Network.

Global Learning Council. (2021). Guidelines for Effective Digital Learning. Global Learning Council.

Google. (2021). Expeditions: Virtual Reality in the Classroom. Google.

Guidi, E. (2011). Benazir income support program: Impact assessment. Pakistan Journal of Social Sciences, 31(2), 45-59.

Hamilton, S. F., & Rahman, T. (2021). Sustainable agricultural practices and their benefits. Journal of Sustainable Agriculture Research, 45(1), 32-47.

Hattie, J., & Timperley, H. (2007). The power of feedback. Review of Educational Research, 77(1), 81-112.

IBM. (2022). Watson Education: Transforming Learning with AI. IBM.

Iqbal, M. A., & Khan, I. A. (2020). Decision making in sustainable agriculture. Journal of Agricultural Science and Technology, 20(1), 45-59.

ISTE. (2016). ISTE Standards for Students. International Society for Technology in Education.

Johnson, L., & Adams Becker, S. (2017). Horizon Report: 2017 Higher Education Edition. New Media Consortium.

Johnson, R., & Lee, S. (2019). The role of AI in personalized education. Journal of Educational Technology & Society, 22(3), 123-136.

Knewton. (2022). Adaptive Learning Technology. Knewton.

Korean Ministry of Education. (2021). SMART Education Initiative. Korean Ministry of Education.

Kusnandar, B., & Rahmat, A. (2019). Sustainable agricultural practices in Southeast Asia. Journal of Environmental Management, 22(1), 45-59.

Lawless, K. A., & Pellegrino, J. W. (2007). Professional development in integrating technology into teaching and learning. Review of Educational Research, 77(4), 575-614.

Loizou, E., & Smith, M. (2019). Agriculture's role in economic development. Journal of Agricultural Economics, 45(2), 78-91.

Los Angeles Times. (2014). LAUSD iPad Program. Los Angeles Times.

Magsi, H. (2014). Review of rural development programs in Pakistan. Journal of Rural Development & Administration, 25(3), 89-105.

MIT Media Lab. (2021). Digital Certificates Project. MIT Media Lab.

MacRae, R. J., Hill, S. B., Henning, J., & Mehuys, G. R. (1990). Agricultural science and sustainable agriculture: A review of the existing scientific barriers to sustainable food production and potential solutions. Biological Agriculture & Horticulture, 7(3), 173-219.

Ministry of Education Singapore. (2021). ICT Masterplans in Education. Ministry of Education Singapore.

Ministry of Education Singapore. (2022). FutureSchools@Singapore. Ministry of Education Singapore.

Miller, A. (2022). Blockchain for educational credentials: Opportunities and challenges. Journal of Higher Education Policy and Management, 44(1), 23-36.

Ministry of Education Singapore. (2021). Smart Learning Spaces. Ministry of Education Singapore.

Munir, A., & Umar, F. (2010). Government objectives in agriculture and food security in Pakistan. Pakistan Journal of Agricultural Research, 31(4), 123-135.

Nordic Innovation. (2022). AI in Finnish Education. Nordic Innovation.

Nair, P. K. R., & Garrity, D. (2021). Agroforestry for sustainable development. Journal of Forestry Research, 22(3), 341-356.

Niroula, B. (2021). Impact of British colonial policies on Indian agriculture. Journal of Historical Studies, 19(2), 123-138.

OECD. (2021). The Impact of Digital Learning on Education Outcomes. OECD.

Open Source Initiative. (2021). The Benefits of Open Source in Education. Open Source Initiative.

Padda, I. U. H., & Hameed, S. (2018). Food security policies and programs in Pakistan. Journal of Social Science Policy Review, 12(1), 23-34.

Plan Ceibal. (2020). One Laptop per Child: Bridging the Digital Divide. OLPC.

Qureshi, A. S. (2011). Water management in agriculture: New paradigms. Journal of Water Resource Management, 23(4), 567-579.

Rahman, S., & Zhang, Z. (2018). Adoption of sustainable agricultural practices in developing countries. Journal of Agricultural Research, 19(2), 65-79.

Razzaq, A., & Smith, J. (2022). Water markets and their impact on agricultural water use efficiency. Journal of Environmental Economics, 23(2), 134-149.

Rocketship. (2021). Blended Learning at Rocketship Public Schools. Rocketship Education.

Routroy, S., & Behera, A. (2017). Barriers to sustainable agriculture in developing countries. Journal of Agricultural Extension and Rural Development, 9(8), 148-157.

Sampatrao, R. (2020). British colonial irrigation projects in India. Journal of Historical Studies, 20(3), 87-103.

Shah, S. A. A., & Shafique, M. (2019). The role of agriculture in Pakistan's economy. Pakistan Journal of Agricultural Research, 32(2), 101-116.

Shokat, S., & Großkinsky, D. K. (2019). The potential of sustainable agriculture in addressing food security challenges in Pakistan. Journal of Agricultural Science and Technology, 21(1), 23-34.

Sikandar, S., & Ahmad, M. (2022). Challenges and prospects of sustainable agriculture in Pakistan. Journal of Agricultural Economics and Development, 43(1), 98-113.

Slijper, E., & Vos, C. (2023). Institutional values and sustainable agriculture practices. Journal of Agricultural Sustainability, 34(2), 112-130.

Smith, J., & Jones, M. (2020). Professional Development for Digital Learning. Educational Technology Research and Development.

Smith, M., & Brown, J. (2022). Ethical considerations in educational technology. Journal of Educational Ethics, 25(2), 76-89.

Suess-Reyes, J., & Fuetsch, E. (2016). Theoretical foundations of sustainable agriculture. Journal of Sustainable Agriculture, 5(2), 35-48.

Swedish Ministry of Education. (2021). National Digital Strategy for Schools. Swedish Ministry of Education.

Taylor, J., Johnson, R., & Lee, S. (2022). Future Trends in Educational Technology. Journal of Educational Technology Research, 45(3), 123-136.

Thompson, D. (2021). Addressing diverse learning needs through VR and AR. Journal of Educational Technology Systems, 49(1), 87-101.

Trigo, E., Cap, E. J., & Maluf, R. S. (2021). The role of sustainable agriculture in achieving global development goals. Agricultural Systems, 183, 102-113.

UK Department for Education. (2021). Educational Technology Agency Proposal. UK Department for Education.

University of California. (2021). Smart Campus Initiative. University of California.

UNESCO. (2021). Bridging the Digital Divide in Education. UNESCO.

Upadhyay, R. K. (2019). Sustainable agriculture in India: A historical perspective. Journal of Agricultural Research, 27(1), 23-34.

Uziak, J., & Lorencowicz, E. (2017). Perceptions and realities of sustainable agriculture in developing countries. Journal of Rural Development, 35(4), 89-101.

Velten, S. (2014). Adaptive management in sustainable agriculture. Journal of Sustainable Agriculture, 6(3), 45-59.

Williams, P. (2018). Educational applications of VR and AR. Journal of Interactive Learning Research, 29(4), 645-662.

Yaqoob, M., Shahzad, M., & Ahmed, N. (2022). Factors influencing the adoption of sustainable agricultural practices. Journal of Agricultural Extension and Rural Development, 14(1), 12-23.

Yeong Sheng Tey, Y. & Li, C. (2017). Risk management in sustainable agriculture: Evaluating adaptation strategies. Journal of Agricultural Sustainability, 8(4), 234-246.

Zulfiqar, F., & Thapa, G. B. (2017). Green revolution and its impact on sustainable agriculture in Pakistan. Journal of Agricultural Research, 21(2), 87-99.

YOUR KNOWLEDGE HAS VALUE

- We will publish your bachelor's and
  master's thesis, essays and papers

- Your own eBook and book -
  sold worldwide in all relevant shops

- Earn money with each sale

Upload your text at www.GRIN.com
and publish for free